An Idler on the Shropshire Borders

BY

Ida Gandy

Illustrations by David Jones

ALAN SUTTON
1989

ALAN SUTTON PUBLISHING
BRUNSWICK ROAD · GLOUCESTER

First published in 1970 by
Wilding and Son Limited, Shrewsbury

This edition published in 1989

British Library Cataloguing in Publication Data

Gandy, Ida
    An idler on the Shropshire borders.
    1.   Shropshire. Rural regions. Social life,
    1910–1945. Biographies
    I.   Title
    942.4'5063'0924

ISBN 0–86299–592–2

Cover picture: A Figure by a Cottage *by Carrier-Belleuse.*
Photograph: The Bridgeman Art Gallery.

Printed in Great Britain by
The Guernsey Press Company Limited,
Guernsey, Channel Islands.

Contents

Biographical Introduction

Ida Gandy (née Hony) was born in 1885. Her paternal ancestors had been for generations parsons or landowners, often both, first in Cornwall and later in Wiltshire. Her grandfather was a fellow of Exeter College, Oxford, held one of the college livings and later became Archdeacon of Sarum, living partly in the close at Salisbury. He was an enthusiastic botanist, geologist and archaeologist. His son, Ida's father, was vicar of Bishop's Cannings near Devizes and later of neighbouring Woodborough. Her mother's family were engineers, builders and timber merchants; Ida's maternal grandfather, Stephen Lewin, was a keen student of church architecture. When only twenty-one he published a book illustrated by himself on Lincolnshire churches; later he submitted a design for the Albert Memorial and designed and made railway engines. Emphatically not the typical parson's wife of the 1880s, his daughter could not sew a button on straight or sing a hymn in tune; she allowed the children to run barefoot and put the girls into serge knickers instead of the then correct white frilly drawers. She frequently entered literary competitions in the newspapers and once won a prize with a review of a play she had never seen.

Her daughter Ida was always a compulsive writer. Another of her enthusiasms was for social reform. After a short semi-academic stay in Oxford with a University family, she set off to undertake social work in London – again, not the conventional choice for a young girl of good family. A job with the Workers' Educational Association took her to Peppard in south Oxfordshire where she met the local GP, Dr Thomas Gandy, whom she married in 1915. He became Chairman of the local Labour Party – even less 'the thing' in those days.

Dr Gandy and his wife stayed in Peppard for fifteen years and had three children. Mrs Gandy began to write and stage plays for the local amateurs, some of which were published and widely performed. She also wrote children's books; her *Three Bold Explorers*, based on the childhood experiences of herself and her siblings, was followed in 1929 by *Sunset Island*, in which legendary supernatural figures – Kelpies, Boggarts, Leprechauns (she had read them all up in the British Museum) – were pictured as surviving together on a distant western island. Then in 1930 came her first well-known book, *A Wiltshire Childhood* (reprinted in 1988 by Alan Sutton Publishing). J.C. Squire published one of her short stories in the *London Mercury*, then the leading literary periodical.

Ida had for years pined for wilder country than the already urbanized landscape of south Oxfordshire and in 1930 she persuaded her husband to move to Clunbury in Shropshire, the surroundings of which provided the background for her next children's book, *Under the Chestnut Tree* (1938). Supported by a cast of villagers from Clunbury she also broadcast from the BBC in Birmingham on Shropshire life.

Bred in the tradition of service to the community cherished by country parsons and doctors, she had long been active in the Women's Institute, and during the Second World War was involved in strenuous work for evacuees and other good causes. In 1945 she and her husband retired to Cerne Abbas in Dorset. He died in 1948 and Mrs Gandy returned to her own county of Wiltshire and settled in Aldbourne near Marlborough.

Her children long since grown up and away from home (to see them she visited Iran, Portugal, Libya and the USA) and her energies unabated, Ida now resumed writing. In 1960 she published *Round About the Little Steeple*, a carefully researched social history of her birthplace, Bishop's Cannings, which was followed in 1963 by *Staying with the Aunts*, a vivid account of her father's family and in particular of her five maiden aunts, survivors from the Victorian age, who lived together and kept their coachman and carriage into the 1920s.

Ida was now approaching eighty but still books came. Her passion for the unspoilt Shropshire landscape led in 1970 to *An Idler on the Shropshire Borders*, a nostalgic volume of description and reminiscence. Her last book, *The Heart of a Village*, about the past and present of Aldbourne, where she had lived since 1950, appeared in 1975 – her ninetieth year. She died in September 1977.

David Jones

CLUNBURY CHURCH

I

FINDING THE VILLAGE

As a summer such as comes only once or twice in a lifetime drew to
a close; as one brilliant day followed another; as lawn and children
alike grew browner and browner, a longing to do something really
exciting before it was over started up in me, grew daily stronger,
and took shape.

So much of England was unknown to me. My newly acquired,
though ancient, Baby Austin, should take me and our two boys
exploring. Jill, a two-year-old daughter, could safely be left with a
kind, capable woman who had recently come to help in the house.
Tom, my doctor husband, though unable to leave his practice,
gave the plan his blessing, partly because it might further something
he long had in mind—the finding of a new practice. After twenty-one
years he felt the need of a change. Also we both coveted a place
remoter from a big town, a place less tamed and robbed of identity
than our own bit of Southern England was fast becoming. And,
for my husband particularly, to spend his spare time with a fishing-
rod was a cherished ambition. He wanted badly to live beside a river.

I quickly made my plans, and on a morning in mid-August the
three of us, Thomas, Oliver, and myself, started off at sunrise,
with a small tent, a sleeping sack, and a basket of food. A light
haze intensified the feeling that this was a true mystery tour. The
parched Common, the village shop, the faces of various patients,
took on a look of unreality.

I had no firm idea of where we would spend the succeeding
nights. Nevertheless, one bit of England drew me forcibly. This was
the south-west corner of Shropshire adjoining Wales, coloured and
tempting rich brown on my Bartholomew map. In particular my
eye fastened on a small village in the heart of it. It stood beside a
river with high hills all round. The maps of Mr. Bartholomew are
far livelier than the dull, if more efficient, Ordnance surveys.

The difference resembled that between Bentham and Hooker and Anne Pratt's flower-books.

Through another village where more patients looked at us in surprise over their gates, through beech woods still in shadow; across the Thames; up over the downs in a south-westerly direction and past the little church where we once went to look for the reputed tombs of giants. Regretfully we eventually took to the main road near Newbury, through the little market town of Hungerford, and so to Savernake Forest. Once well inside it we sat down, ravenous, for breakfast.

Long ago, as a child, we—my parents and five or six brothers and sisters and myself, some on cycles, some in our old carriage, the Family Ark, used to celebrate my father's April birthday, or my mother's May one, by a picnic in the Forest. Such grand picnics, such wealth of food, such wanderings later into the deeper woodland, where you could often surprise a deer. But never before had I breakfasted there; and though the meal was far below my mother's standard, the old magic returned as we ate our bread-and-butter and hard-boiled eggs.

By the time I had slept in the bracken and the boys lost and found themselves again, the sun had grown very powerful. We packed up and made for another much loved spot—Martinsell—the noble headland at the eastern end of the long line of downs bounding the Pewsey Vale. There I, and other members of my family, had once tobogganed in summer down smooth, burnt grass. And here my sons now did the same, till it seemed little would be left of their knickers. Another picnic, a doze for everyone, then on through Marlborough, over Hackpen, down and up, and down again, through busy harvest fields, and so to Malmesbury. 'Here', I decided, as we crossed the Avon beside the big silk-mill, and looked up at the little grey town, 'we will spend the night'.

This proved easy. We booked beds at the first nice-looking pub, and set off to explore. Though a born Wiltshirewoman I knew nothing of Malmesbury, and was amazed by the beauty and size of the Abbey, and charmed by the way the houses dropped in terraces to the river. The boys played a kind of hide and seek, disappearing and reappearing in different directions through narrow alleys and up and down flights of steps.

A loitering journey next day brought us through the unknown county of Herefordshire to the home of a childhood friend, now married to a fruit farmer on the slopes of some hills near Ledbury. We were at once invited to stay the night, I in the house, the boys to camp with our host's family in their orchard. A last glimpse showed them blissfully happy in the green twilight. I only prayed that not too many of the plums that hung so temptingly above them, or lay in heaps on the ground, would find their way into their mouths.

Almost unwillingly next morning we moved northwards into Shropshire, but always the temptation to linger was defeated by the thought of those deep brown squares of country on our map. Not that there weren't hills enough here—gently flowing hills. But they were all coloured a pale brown. We drove up and down them, beside small rivers, through endless plum and apple orchards, through villages and country towns, delighted all the while by the newness, the beauty, the richness.

In the late afternoon we found ourselves high on the hills to the east of Church Stretton, close to a grand outstanding peak called Caer Caradoc. The weather remained glorious; here we agreed, we would spend the night. All seemed perfect, all seemed made for our pleasure, as we sat to tea among hills so vast and wild after our Oxfordshire homeland. The boys went in search of a pool to paddle in, and I fell happily asleep again. I had lain down bathed in the evening sunlight. I woke to a strangely hostile world. Though still early evening the sky was dark with monstrous clouds backed by a sombre orange glow. How long I slept I don't know but the change was electrifying. From behind the hills sounded a faint muttering of thunder that grew louder moment by moment. The boys came running over the grass in high excitement. We seized our scattered belongings and rushed to the car, but not before the rain was torrential and the thunder deafening. As fast as possible in such conditions, we made for the valley. I hope never again to drive in such a storm. Darkness enveloped us and the lightning flashed with such vigour that I kept on the road with difficulty. Where, oh where, could we now spend the night? But fate was kind. The owners of a small guest house in Church Stretton took us in and gave us supper, also breakfast next morning.

Through a refreshed and sparkling world we drove on under the Long Mynd beside a wooded river, turned west beside a small station, and after a few miles up and down found ourselves beside a signpost marked with the very name I had pin-pointed on my

9

map. There, below us, was the village, so much in harmony with my fancies that I could hardly believe it. A small but solid church tower, half-hidden by trees, a steep, bracken-covered hillside, a few houses and cottages pushing up between orchards and hedgerows, a little river shining among the trees, and above all, hills of every shape and size slipping to the valley. A steep lane and two stone bridges led us first over a stream and then a little river. We were in the village.

At a tiny shop close to the church I asked where I could find a bed for the night and the boys a camping ground. A brisk little woman gave me an appraising glance, said she could take me in herself, and that she felt no doubt the doctor, over the way, would let the boys use his orchard. All was settled in a few minutes. The doctor's wife, a pleasant sandy-haired woman, seemed pleased to have the boys and led us to an orchard on the banks of the river. She also invited me to drink coffee with her that evening.

Directly the tents were disposed of and our landlady had given us tea, we set off up the village street for the high hill that rose steeply on the south. In such a hurry were we to climb it that we ignored the path and swarmed straight up the most precipitous part.

Never shall I forget the effect of the view that burst on us when we reached the top. How truthful Mr. Bartholomew had been when he coloured his map of that part of the world those rich shades of brown! Everywhere hills rose and fell. The river wandered away westwards and was lost in their folds, but eastwards it doubled under our hill to twist on through quiet empty fields in a southerly direction. A particularly fine summit, dark with heather, dominated the western landscape. Further south was a fascinating sharply pointed peak, and still further away a mass of deep blue upland. Further still a pale range dropped sharply as the roof of a house. Even when the land flattened out, fresh hills, big or little, swelled up to catch the evening light. It seemed to me that if one lived in this part there would be a new one to climb every week of the year.

When I had seen the boys lying peacefully under the apple trees, with the river only a yard or two away, I drank coffee at the doctor's house. I cannot remember that our conversation was memorable in any way. But next morning, something of real importance happened. The wife had been showing me round her garden, an adorable garden with many unusual flowers and odd little twists and turns, steps, and arches cut through hedges. When the time came to leave, I said on a sudden impulse, 'Please, if this practice is ever for sale will you let me know?'

Her reply was fateful. 'We put it in the agent's hands last week', she said. It seemed incredible. A practice among these hills; a practice, with it's own trout stream at the foot of the garden, was for sale!

After that fate took its inevitable course. At the earliest possible moment I brought my husband to see for himself. He listened to facts and figures, then wandered down to the river and gazed at it lovingly, noting every small trout that swam by. I for my part looked at the hills. These and the river proved irresistible. We took a big gamble, sold our more lucrative practice and settled into our new house some four months later.

II

SETTLING IN

Three people, the services of two of whom we inherited from our predecessors, wonderfully eased our settling in. Lizzie, pale-faced, black-haired, with soft violet eyes behind spectacles, and an almost supernaturally sweet temper; and Harry Meredith, the gardener (the accent on the second syllable in these parts); and Lily, pale and fair as her name, who lived next door; loved children and volunteered to help in the care of Jill.

Nobody, I think, could better have typified this Border-land than Harry. The stocky strength of the English countryman, his earthiness, his shrewdness, his humour, his independence of spirit, were linked with the dramatic feeling and love of music of a Welshman. Harry possessed a rich tenor voice, and all his family sang like birds.

Church bells were the joy of his life. He was both head ringer and choirmaster, and ready to take a part whenever a play was going. His physical strength was terrific, and he could be formidable on occasion, but never if treated with due respect. He served both as a bulwark and the encyclopedia to which we turned daily for information about this unknown country. 'The Obley?' His broad thumb descended on it. 'Llanbrook? Down there below the Llan. Whittalls? Close under the hill as they can squeeze'.

Without his guidance Tom would have lost himself perpetually in the maze of small lanes that ran up into the heart of the hills. As it was he managed, not without difficulty sometimes, to reach the right house.

Those hills! They proved the undoing of a housewife who had never developed a proper housewifely conscience. Desultory falls of snow soon after our arrival only increased their enchantment.

When we had been in the village for a few days, I ignored the forlorn assembly of odd bits of furniture, the ornaments, the mountains of books, and jumped into Tom's car as he started for his surgery at the neighbouring market town. After a couple of miles I left him and crossed the river. My path led up into woods where I met a plump, jolly girl of sixteen or so gathering sticks. She offered to accompany me wherever I pleased. It was all one to her which way she went as long as she returned with a load of wood. Otherwise her mother would dress her down. We struck up through the trees, and she expressed curiosity as to who I might be. She'd never set eyes on me before, she said.

'No, I've only been here a week. I'm the new doctor's wife'.

'Oh my good Lord!' she exclaimed, 'you a doctor's wife!'

I hardly knew how to take this.

'I've never been to a doctor in my life', she declared, 'but I s'pose one day I'll have to'.

It was very quiet in the woods except for her chatter and the chirp of tits in the tree tops. After a while my companion said she 's'posed she'd better get on with her wooding'. I helped her for a few minutes and then said I would climb to the sky-line to go home along the top of the hills.

'Oh, my good Lord!' she cried again, as though this was a Herculean feat. She seemed amazed when I boasted of the far longer walks I sometimes took.

'But then', she said, 'I guess you keep a maid'. I admitted, not without a slight sense of shame, that such was the case. *I* had time for such things. *She* had not.

When I reached the top of the ridge, snowflakes began to flutter down. But they didn't seem to matter. After the more enclosed country I had known for so long these far-stretching hills seemed heaven; their loneliness, their silence; the snow-charged clouds dropping down on them. Suddenly this silence was broken by a plaintive piping. Among the shadows at the farther side of the field a boy was rounding up some sheep, playing a rambling little tune on a mouth-organ as he strode along. I realised still better that we had come into a musical country.

As soon as the house began to look less forlorn I went up the Hill—that is, our own special hill—in search of snowdrops that Harry told me grew on the further side in a place called Rock Forest. In my eagerness to be off I failed to listen properly to his directions, and struck out too far westwards. Under every hedge and furrow and bank lay bars of snow. The wind, coming straight from the Welsh mountains, was bitter.

No sign of a forest. I dropped to a cottage beside a spring, where a black-eyed young man stood at the door. When I asked for a drink of water he seemed surprised at such a request on such a cold day, but at once drew me a glassful, and then gave me my directions, with sundry bits of information thrown in. His cottage stood highest in the hamlet below us which he said was called the Twitchen. I looked down and saw more little greystone houses, all equally solid and equally rooted on the hillside. I hoped Tom would have many patients here. It seemed such a loveable place. And with that name!

Many foxes ran past his door, he said, on their way between Pursloe Wood, on the other side of the valley, and Rock Forest. He often heard them crying to each other in the night. On that hill yonder—the peaked one, called the Titterhill—you could pick all the whinberries you wanted. O yes, it was grand country in *summer*. Further than that he refused to go.

Following his directions I went southwards till I saw the dark tops of fir trees ahead. The Forest (some might call it only a wood, but I was glad it was called a forest) lay in a deep hollow. Through the middle ran a tiny stream buried under a mass of bracken. The firs gave place to gnarled hawthorns and elders covered with Jews' Ears, and there were many birds' nests, all full of snow. Underneath grew the snowdrops, hundreds of them. Only a few sleepy, disgruntled blackbirds and the sharp crack of sticks a little lower down broke the stillness. Peeping through the bushes I saw the shadowy figure of an old woman snapping them over her knee. I hurried home before I should lose my way in the gathering darkness, happy at the discovery of a place to come to over and over again.

The river—or rather the Brook as they all called it here—offered almost as much temptation as the hills. All my life I had wished for a nearby hill to climb, and a river to wander by. Now I had both. The Brook, big enough to be exciting, small enough to adopt for one's own, filled my need exactly. Plans for a small boat, for family bathing, for picnics, sprang to mind. At first the bitter wind always made me hurry along the banks, but one evening the air blew so soft and kind through the open window that Tom and I got up from our tea and wandered out across the orchard to the Brook. It was then I met my first dippers. They were sitting together on a bough just above the water, bowing gently, white bibs gleaming in the dusk. From that moment they became one of my favourite birds. The Hill appeared now a huge shadow against the sky and a star leaped up behind it. Then the sound of church bells ringing a muffled peal floated across the village street and over the fields. We knew from Harry whom they commemorated—a young sailor from the village who had just died in a Russian port from smallpox. Everyone here had loved him. He rang the bells himself as soon as he could grasp a rope; he sang in the choir; as a child he constantly paddled in the Brook. And now here were we, making it a part of *our* life, just as *his* had ended. The bells, now confident and vigorous, now muted and melancholy, symbolised the difference.

Not long after our arrival a sale at a small farm among the hills gave me a vivid glimpse of the people we had come to live among. The farmer had recently died and his widow was selling out. On the way I picked up a retired shepherd whom I had seen in the surgery. He had that simple friendly manner I noted in all the people around.

He didn't want to buy anything himself, he said, 'but I be gwaine because owd Bill was a pal of mine'. As I soon discovered, these sales are great social events. It's as much a matter of courtesy to attend a neighbour's sale as his funeral. As we drove on up the steep little road that led into the hills we passed small groups all making for the farm as fast as their legs, or their ponies, or their bicycles, or ancient cars, could carry them. Most of them brought baskets of food, which they later ate in the cottage kitchen, or in the yard while they waited for the sale to begin.

According to my friend you must never expect a sale to begin at the advertised hour, and in this case it did not start till two o'clock —an hour late. But while we waited the arrival of the auctioneer we poked our noses about among the goods piled up in the yard and garden. A most miscellaneous collection it was, comprising among other things a churn, milk-tins, a pony-trap, a huge side of bacon, hen-coops, household furniture and crockery. Inside the house was the oak corner-cupboard which was the ostensible reason for my coming. I had always longed for a corner-cupboard. A continuous burble of friendly greetings filled the air, such as, 'Why, Bill, I hanna set eyes on 'ee for a twelve month. Where you bin hidin' yerself?' 'Why Tom, thought ee'd sold yerself long with your sheep last Michaelmas'.

Many of the men were of racy type, with faces which, if not handsome, were strongly individual, shrewd, or humorous. Many wore faded velveteen jackets and brightly coloured scarves round their necks. One old fellow, who arrived on a stout pony, had a particularly amusing face, with plump rosy cheeks, busy side whiskers, a big globular nose and tiny pig-like eyes.

Suddenly there was a stir and a bustle. The auctioneer, a dashing young man with blue eyes and weather-beaten face, had arrived and was taking hasty survey of the goods he was to sell.

A few minutes later he got to work in the yard. This was the men's side of the affair and nearly all the women, except a few very determined ones, were elbowed out. Bidding for the side of bacon was very brisk. There was 55 lbs. of it and it eventually fell to a lean, red-haired farmer, who looked as though he needed it, at elevenpence a pound. People from the nearby hamlet of Obley secured so many bargains that someone remarked, 'Reckon they've got all the money at Obley'.

'Aye', answered an Obley man, 'Twas blown up here in the last gale and stuck on the fence on the top of the hill'. Loud guffaws of laughter.

Among the crowd of country people, I noticed a little couple who seemed like myself to be newcomers to this part of the world.

The man, about 5 ft. 3 in., had a bushy grey moustache and eyebrows, the woman, shorter than he, wore nice dowdy clothes and had small twinkling eyes that sized us all up in a kindly fashion.

When we got pushed close together she said, 'Our name is McCroben. We've recently come to the village. I hope we may be friends as well as neighbours'. I felt sure we should.

Among the furniture was a queer little spinning chair with a tiny seat and tall back. A facetious old man suggested to an enormous woman with three chins that it might suit her.

'My God, no!' she exclaimed. 'Only one corner of me would get on it'.

The widow of the farmer whose property was being sold showed great activity, poking her wrinkled face in and out among the crowd and watching with alert eyes auctioneer and bidders alike. She wore a man's old felt hat on her sandy hair and was enveloped in a blue overall. When anything seemed likely to go for too low a price her sharp little eyes burned with indignation, and she would fix them on the prospective buyer as though to say, 'Now then, be a gentleman! Bid up, man, bid up!'

When we moved from the yard to the furniture and crockery in the house the women came into their own. I noticed that many were far more careful about money than the men, and that they usually refused to raise the bid by more than threepence at a time. One old lady with a huge pale face and a mouth that gaped like a fish's must, I thought, be disconcerting to the auctioneer, for after she had reached her limit—which she indicated by closing her lips tightly for a second or two—her mouth continued to open and close spasmodically, recording other people's bids.

Owing to my lack of experience I failed to make my bid at the right moment and lost the corner-cupboard. But that didn't matter terribly; the sale had been as good as a play. When at last it was all over the crowd stayed on to discuss their bargains and to continue an exchange of local gossip. The women, in particular, were out to make a day of it.

As I drove the old shepherd back down the valley the hills were soft and blurry under the east wind, and the air full of the bleating of sheep and lambs. Once again I said to myself, 'How glad I am we came to these parts'.

III

THE PARISH

The Village

Sometimes you meet people who raise high hopes at first sight, but who prove so bound by custom, so lacking in all adventurousness, that you never get beyond smiles, friendly words, and an invitation to tea.

It is the same with places. They may look pretty and alluring with a suggestion that they have still more to offer when you know them better. But somehow, for you at all events, the suggestion is never fulfilled.

Our village was not like that. The happy anticipation that filled me when first I pin-pointed it on the map, had been a true one. Throughout the fifteen years that we were to spend there, she, and the surroundings that helped to make her what she was, gave out an ever-deepening reward. Her situation in the long, winding river valley, at the foot of her own special hill; the other hills that raised blue, green, brown, or purple heads in all directions; the way the church stood boldly above the river; all these endeared her to me. Moreover, in the twelfth-century tower hung six good bells, and I had grown up to the sound of bells. Harry was a truly consecrated ringer, who trained the young to follow in his footsteps.

'All bells have their own words', he said. 'Ours are—"Our old cow'n got a long tail". Over the hill they ask "Who sings best?" and Little Hopton Castle answers, "We two".

Clun has more bells, so—
> "Drop it and run,
> Say the bells of Clun".'

Just outside the church was the little shop, which a year or two later would be taken over by Harry and his handsome, loveable wife. Once there had been a small pub beside the church-gate, but now the nearest was the Hundred House, half-a-mile across the fields. A procession of cottages and houses ran up the street, with orchards and gardens opening on to wide water meadows. Below ours rose the tall old Mill House, formerly combined with a carpenter's shop. Above us the blacksmith worked from dawn to dusk at a forge owned by his family since the 16th century. The principle farmhouse, a strong fine-looking place, stood just above the river, and to this farm belonged most of the meadows round, and also a large portion of sheep-grazing on the Hill. The farmer, a dour, elderly man, rode about on a shaggy pony. Apart from his farm he was chiefly interested in archaeology, and he would sometimes return from the Hill with a pocketful of flints. Long ago there must have been a flint factory up there and the children often brought well-worked flints for their school museum.

This old farmer was uncommon close in his ways, people told us. He sold skim milk to his men at a penny a pint, and one day when a labourer offered sixpence for a week's payment, the farmer's wife cried, 'Gracious, William, that's a bad sixpence!'

'Well, m'am', answered he, 'tis what master gave *me* last week'. The wife, one of the least reticent people I had ever met, told the story herself. She was dark, loquacious, and amusing, both intentionally and unintentionally. But she was truly alive and truly kind, though also observant of other people's foibles. The stories she told often kept us shaking with laughter.

A much humbler farm, Chapel Farm, on the opposite side of the river, supplied us with milk. The house had been a Chapel till strange sounds were heard coming from it at night. The Devil himself haunted it, said the congregation; so they refused to worship there any longer. Fortunately no more was heard of him when it became a farm. Two of its fields, lying between the Clun and its tributary, the Kemp, were named the Hop-Field and the Vineyard. The farmer was a sad-looking man with side-whiskers and few words. His daughter was married just after our first hay harvest, but the poor man grieved so much at losing her that he would not go to the church. Instead he stayed working all day on top of the rick. Even when the bells pealed out and the bride—looking charming in a dress of birds-eye blue—came down the lane and over the footbridge, he scarcely raised his eyes, but continued his job as though nothing was happening. Later on the wedding guests sauntered across the meadow to the river bank with chairs, and there they sat singing songs and listening to a gramophone. But still the poor father worked on with gloomy face till it was too dark to see any more.

Some people lived in the most remote places. One day I set off to find the home of a valiant little woman who, wet or fine, never failed to turn up at our W.I. I marvelled at her energy as I climbed one steep field after another till at last I reached her cottage at the head of a little valley beside a stream. It was called 'The Backs', and certainly belonged to the kind of country known as 'The Back of Beyond'. Three tabby cats sat in the sun on the doorstep, and a young nanny goat emerged from a little house beautifully built of logs, bracken and broom. She seemed pleased to see me, and nozzled me in a friendly way. But sad to say her owner was out.

There were many others living on top of the hills, or down in small valleys, or up steep lanes of whom I shall say something later.

At the top of the village street lived an old woman known as 'Granny Hughes', who wanted me to visit her. I went, in torrents of rain, and found her sitting in a dark little room on the edge of her bed, propped up by pillows. She refused to get inside it by day for fear of growing bedridden, yet, because of her rheumatism and the steep stairs she could never join her son and his family below in the kitchen. I asked her to tell me about her early life, which most old people love to do. It is a release from the present, even if it is the tale of a hard life such as hers. She was born a few miles away under a high hill called Caer Caradoc (not the one opposite the Long Mynd), where her father owned a small farm. Though her mother had nine children she yet managed to keep a little school in the farmhouse kitchen when there was no compulsory education. This was about 1860, I reckoned. The pupils came from other farms up in the hills and stayed all day.

'My mother used to give them hot stew for their dinner in front of the fire. I do seem to see her still ladlin' it out', she said. 'They didna come so much in summer because of the farm work. My mother was always happy and smiling, but she died when she was only thirty-six. Wore out, the poor dear soul.

'We was very happy there, while we had her', she went on. 'We'd spend half the day on the hill. Or we climbed about in the oakwoods on t'other side of the valley, till mother found out they was sniving with adders'. She used this expressive word, new to me, again when she spoke of a house 'sniving' with rats.

Her own husband fell off a ladder at Guilden Down, where he worked on a farm, and in falling bit his tongue so hard that a cancer started. He lived on for eleven years in great misery, ten shillings a week being the amount of compensation allowed him. With thirteen children to keep she was forced to work as school-cleaner, and often she picked swedes and turnips in the fields. At night there was all the family washing, ironing and mending to be done, and she seldom got to bed before eleven or twelve. Then by five o'clock next morning she came down to prepare breakfast for the boys who must be off to their work. My goodness, the things the poor have put up with all through the ages!

Yet there was no hint of bitterness in her soft voice, as she sat in the cheerless little room, while the rain beat noisily on the corrugated roof. But she did find the days 'martal long' and loved to be read to. I thought I would try Mrs. Ewing's *Daddy Darwin's Dovecot* on her. When I finished it, she said, 'That bit about the workhouse boy coming to live with the old ladies minds me of summut that happened at Knighton work'hus when I was a child. There was a terrible mischievous boy there, and nothing could daunt him. So at last the Master thought to break his spirit by shutting him up in the dead-house with the coffin of a boy who had died the previous day. But even this didna daunt him. What did he do but open the coffin, take out the dead boy, dress him up in his own clothes and prop him up against the rail at the head of the stairs. Next he wrapped himself in the winding sheet and lay down in the coffin. When t'was growing dark up the stairs comes the Master with some victuals, sees the dead boy standing there and holds the plate out to him, thinking, you see, t'was the live boy. Well, there he stands saying nothing, and the Master looking at him surprised because he did think he'd be hungry by that time, when up from the coffin springs the live boy, wrapped in the white sheet, and cries out in a loud voice, "If he wunna eat it I will!" And the Master was so scared that he fell backward down the stairs and well-nigh broke his neck. Now weren't that a terrible thing?' But I said I thought it served him right.

As she finished this dreadful tale Flossie, her little grand-daughter, came running into the room with a young robin. Soon it slipped through her fingers and flew out of the window. But Flossie remained, rosy and bright-eyed.

Granny Hughes told me a still grimmer story when I brought her a bunch of snowdrops picked in Pursloe Woods. Her eyes brightened at the sight, but a brooding look followed, and after a few minutes she said, 'You picked 'em in Pursloe Woods? Summut dreadful happened in them woods fifty year ago. There was an unmarried girl had a little girl two or three years old. One day she come home from Knighton Market without her, and when the neighbours asked, "Where be the child?" she told them she'd met a lady at Hopton Heath station who took a fancy to it and said as she'd like to adopt it and take it off her hands. And after that she went away to Manchester. Some months later a man who was ploughing in the field just above the wood where the snowdrops grow, went through the gate "to wait on himself" and smelt a terrible smell.

' "Bill", he shouts to his mate, "reckon there must be a corpse somewhere hereabouts".

'So Bill joined him and in among the briars they found some bits of clothing and then further in still the body of the little girl, that fell to pieces when they went to lift it up. So word was sent to the police and one night when the mother was a'bed the bell peals and there they stands at the door.

'And she says "I know what you've come about", and goes with them as quiet as a lamb. She got ten years, but was let out a bit earlier on account of good conduct. Why she got rid of the child was never known, but folk said the father had promised to marry her if so be she could find a home for the little girl. Now war'nt that a dreadful thing that she should leave her own child alone up there in the woods—to die?'

Here was a second Hetty Sorrel, only she received more lenient treatment for a far worse offence. It was in truth a terrible tale, and I was glad when, after Granny had sat silent a moment, her dark old eyes brooding over the past, she spoke of more cheerful things. For she kept a store of memories hoarded up like pieces for a patchwork quilt, some sombre, some gaily-coloured. Had I heard tell of the monstrous great pike that had been gobbling up the fish in the Brook for a long while, till her son Jack went down at night with a lantern and a pitch fork, 'ticed him up with the light, and then stuck him through with the pitch-fork. Thirty pound or more he weighed, Jack said. Doctor 'ull be glad that owd fish be gone, wanna he?'

And had I been yet to Lady Dancing Well over in Brampton Park? Well then, I did ought to go for there was so much iron in the water that if you dropped a pin there 'tis said it 'ull never sink but go spinning round and round. How it be now I dunna rightly know but in my young days folk would come from miles away to collect some of the water in a bottle 'cos of the goodness in it'.

The little couple I had met at the sale proved to be made of true country stuff, even if an urban job had claimed them for much of their working years. He had been a master at a boys public school. Like ourselves they had fallen in love with the village. The country did not mean, for them, just a place where dogs could be freely exercised and a pretty garden cultivated. It meant, for her at all events, roaming the fields and hills, and, for both of them, a close involvement in the life of the village. Their garden, it so happened, was a joy, no tameness, no over-tidiness. Flowers, fruit bushes, and vegetables kept each other close company. At the bottom an orchard harboured Mrs. Mac's Rhode Island Reds and here both of them, in big straw hats with black veils, tended four bee-hives. When we first knew them they were in process of turning vegetarian, largely because Mrs. Mac loathed taking life. She would not even kill wasps when they interrupted her jam-making, and if a bee stung herself or anyone else she was far more concerned about the bee's death than the effects of the sting on a human being. The fruit trees and the roses remained unsprayed but always, in their season, weighted with fruit and flowers. The raspberries packed together in a miniature forest, never failed to produce a mass of berries.

Sausages. These presented their most formidable obstacle to true vegetarianism. 'Frank does so love sausages', she sighed.

Frank grunted. 'Don't pretend, that you don't too, Mary'.

She admitted it sadly, twitching her lips like a rabbit in the way she had. His bushy eyebrows shot up and down as he talked. When he disapproved of anything he would give a snort, particularly when he thought the vicar was preaching too long a sermon, or had made some foolish observation. When he told us from the pulpit that the test of a good book consisted in the number of times it could be read, and that he himself had read *Gone With the*

Wind three times, which showed what a good book it was, Mac's snort was audible right down the church.

There was another snort that I remember well. Mrs. R., a very fat lady, had driven over to tea with the Macs from a neighbouring village in her donkey cart, which she deposited in our barn. The donkey, a sad little creature, still harnessed to the shafts, looked old and underfed. Mrs. R. dismissed any suggestion that he should be loosed and given refreshment, but Jill took him apples and a cabbage leaf.

After four hours Mrs. R. came along to prepare for her homeward journey, accompanied by her hosts with a cockerel that she had just bought from them. When she had thrust him in a basket under the seat she heaved her vast body into the cart and grasped the reins. A tremor ran through the poor little donkey, and his ears twitched.

I gave him an encouraging pat and asked, 'What's his name?' 'He has none', she answered. She gave him a smart blow with her stick and shouted 'Get on!'

At that moment misgivings about the cockerel's comfort seized Mrs. Mac. 'Is he alright like that, do you think?' she asked anxiously. Mrs. R. assumed that Mrs. Mac was concerned for her personal comfort and declared that he was not in her way. As she passed through the gate Mac gave so loud a snort that it surely must have reached her ears. Mrs. Mac expressed her feelings in a long-drawn sigh.

'Twenty years that little creature has pulled her fat body along, and she has never ever given him a name!'

'Four hours', muttered Mac with another snort. 'Four long hours that woman has sat talking about herself! Don't you ever ask her again, Mary'.

Mary promised she never would.

During my fifteen years' close friendship, only once was it sorely tried. The cause—a Rhode-Island cock. Mrs. Mac's mature, handsome bird grew dissatisfied with his rather dowdy, ageing harem, and constantly flew over the wall to enjoy the company of my younger, more attractive hens, and even spent the night with them sometimes. This habit annoyed my own cock, who, though equally handsome and vigorous, was often made aware by the interloper that he was an inferior juvenile, and consequently he would go off moping by himself. One day I noticed only a single cock at feeding time, and concluded that Mrs. Mac's bird had ceased his unwelcome visits. But soon Mrs. Mac arrived and asked 'Have you seen my cock?'

I said, 'Of course I've seen him only too often, but not during the last day or two'.

Mrs. Mac cast a sharp look at *my* cock, buttoned and unbuttoned her mouth, and went away muttering to herself.

The next day I returned from an outing to find no cock among my hens. This seemed extremely suspicious, but it was too late to do anything that night. Next morning, as I was making dumplings, in came Mrs. Mac. She sat down by the fire and waited for me to speak.

'*My* cock has gone', I said.

After much working of her lips she replied, 'He was *my* cock. I took him home yesterday evening'.

'But how do you know he is *your* cock? They are exactly alike'.

'My cock has a specially good tail'.

'So has mine'.

'And a splendid comb'.

'So has mine'.

'And well developed spurs'.

It was all I could do not to fling a dumpling at her.

'So has mine'.

But nothing I could say would convince her that the cock, now shut firmly into her own hen-house, didn't belong to her. Mine must have wandered off and been eaten by a fox.

'Why not *yours*?' I asked.

'Mine would never let himself be eaten. He is a stronger, and altogether more powerful a character'.

I busied myself with my dumplings. Again my fingers itched. She rose and walked out after this final shot.

I decided that I could not continue the fight, but it left a shadow between us for a while. Later on, when the shadow had lifted, I thought how much more time Mrs. Mac spent pottering among her hens than I did, and that her familiarity with them was therefore greater than mine.

Tom had two old patients who live on what is called 'the Mountain'—a remote spot, north of the Ludlow road, and he wanted me to meet them. To reach their cottage we drove up steep narrow lanes, praying we'd meet nothing. The two old men were enthroned beside their door on upturned sugar boxes, smoking their pipes and looking well content with life, though one pressed his tummy in a comical fashion.

'Her's been giving a bit of trouble', he said. 'Wants a drop more of that medicine'. Tom ready armed, produced a bottle and took him inside. The other one busied himself in getting ready the cup of tea that they always gave my husband, while I wandered round looking at the view across the Teme to Stokesay Castle and the wooded hills beyond. A rather rickety chair was brought out for me, Tom sat on a stump, and the old men on their thrones, while we sipped our tea. These two 'did' for themselves, and never troubled much about the inside of their cottage so long as the sun shone and they could sit there looking out on the world. And when it was cold or wet, they piled up an enormous fire with wood they collected in kinder weather.

As we returned through Aston-on-Clun, I noticed that the old tree had been newly decked with a fresh supply of the flags of all nations. These are hung up every year on May 29th, to commemorate the wedding of the squire's daughter over 200 years ago.

The Twitchen

That first glimpse of the Twitchen made me quickly seek a better acquaintance with it, and this came through an old man called Chapman.

As I stood at our gate one day with Harry, a funny little figure buttoned up in a tight frockcoat, green with age, and a bowler hat went past. He wore a small close-clipped moustache and his eyes looked neither to the right or the left. He carried himself with stiff careful precision.

'That's Mr. Chapman from the Twitchen', said Harry. 'Used to be a Ship Steward. A rum old chap, and a hard drinker. Up at the Hundred House he likes to walk round with a glass of whisky on top of his hat. "There", he'll say, "I couldn't do that if I was drunk, could I?" The truth is he couldn't do it if he was sober!'

The next day I went to call on Mr. Chapman in a solid little house as prim as himself. His family had lived there for 200 years he said. He was chopping sticks in the garden, still wearing his bowler, which remained on his head when he took me into his

26

kitchen. This was scrupulously clean and tidy but contained to my sorrow a stuffed otter in a glass case. After a few minutes of reserve he began to talk of his past life in a clipped, formal way that exactly matched his appearance. 'It was the Brook made me want to go to sea', he said. 'I was forever beside it or in it. My mother often thrashed me for walking about in the water with my boots, but it never stopped me. I learned to swim too, and to tickle trout'.

'That otter?' I said. 'Tell me about it. I tried so hard to see one for myself'.

'Ah', he said slowly, with what sounded like real regret, 'I was down by the Kemp at dusk where it serpentines a bit, and suddenly I saw her round the next bend, whistling to her young. Before I'd time to think up went my gun and that was the end of her. 'Twas a pity'.

It was indeed, but as a boy's unpremeditated deed less shocking than the ruthless hunting down of this beautiful creature by hard-faced men and women with their frightful blue uniforms, red stockings and notched sticks, each notch marking a cruel death. He turned to his sea-faring days, and told me he had been twice round the world: to Australia, to India, to China. Couldn't ever sleep in his feather bed when he came home.

''Twas too soft, and I missed the noise of the sea and the creaking of the machinery, I'd wake reg'lar every four hours for the watch'.

When I was about to leave, he said with solemn pride, 'There's something in this old chest I'll show you'.

He opened a drawer and drew out an immense linen table-cloth yellow with age, but of exquisite texture. He passed his fingers over it lovingly and said, 'That was made from flax grown in the garden here, spun by my mother and woven by a travelling weaver. Afterwards we helped carry it out to bleach on the hillside. I mind the day still'. With all those memories woven into it it seemed to me a wonderful possession.

When I visited old Chapman a second time he told me in his dry, precise way that when George III was King his great-aunt planted an acorn in the garden. She tended it carefully and it grew into a fine tree. A few years ago he had it cut down and made into coffin boards for himself. Beautiful boards, he said. 'Yes', Harry told me, 'and now they're in the hands of his special crony, Bert Lewis. From time to time he walks up on a Sunday morning to see how they're weathering—or so he says. The truth is the old chap's

27

afraid they might be used for someone else. He runs his fingers over them blessed boards and says, "Measure me up, Bert", and Bert stands the boards up beside him to make sure they're still the right length'.

Old Chapman certainly deepened my interest in the Twitchen, which continued to fascinate me. It consisted of about twenty houses, some perched on narrow terraces on the steep hillside, each with a spring beside the door; some set along the fringe of a big meadow backed by woods.

A little Chapel stood on the hillside, and close by in a house three or four hundred years old, lived Mrs. Griffiths, a fine type of countrywoman, with a rugged face, sturdy independence of spirit, and an intimate knowledge and love for the Twitchen. Indeed, she seemed as much a part of it as her own house. She had a lame daughter, with serene blue eyes set very wide apart, who was an exquisite needlewoman. She promised to teach Jill to sew one day. I may say that when the time came she could scarcely have had a more rebellious, uninterested pupil. Yet all the same they got on well together.

This old house had sheltered very different occupants some eighty years before. It was standing empty and in need of repairs when a gang of poachers and sheep stealers made it their head-quarters. 'A real desperate lot they were', her father told Mrs. Griffiths. 'One man would bide in the house and signal to his mates, who had hid themselves under Pursloe Wood, by hanging a sheet from the window to show when the ground was clear. Then off to the woods they'd creep with their guns, and each would mark his bird. Not a soul dared stop 'em, for like as not they'd a bin shot themselves'.

At other times the gang would be off over the hills after sheep. They were such a wild, crafty lot that they never got caught. But things grew too hot for them at last, and they disappeared. After that the cottage had a very different occupant. This was an old woman called Isabella Pearce, who gathered herbs from the hillside, the woods, the fields, the hedges, and made them into medicines and ointments.

'Powerful good they were, my mother said, so that customers came from miles around. When I was a child I remember seeing the old lady wandering about in a grey cloak, talking to herself, and stooping to pick this and that. For one of her charms she used the Briar-boss. You know what I mean, the little red, furry ball that grows on briars?'

'Robin's pin-cushion is the name I know', I said.

'Well', Isabella declared, 'if you han the tuthache and you light on a Briar-boss accidental, and you wear 'un in your buzzom it'll cure 'un'.

'Perhaps because it would so irritate your "buzzom" that you'd forget the toothache', I suggested.

'Come to think of it that well might be', agreed Mrs. Griffiths. 'Once', she continued, 'there were big plantations up behind the Twitchen, but they were all cut down for charcoal-burning. You can still see three black patches left by the fires. And there were three wells up there, once used by the charcoal burners. They got lost, and the farmer asked a water-diviner to find one so that the sheep might not go thirsty. And he did'.

Mrs. Griffiths remembered a toll-gate where Redwood Lane, that ran east from the Twitchen and was once an old coaching road, joined up with the present main road. An old woman—wide as her door—lived in the toll-house. She was slow on her feet, but 'My word! She'd be out in a jiffy when a toll was to be took—6d. for a horse in harness, 3d. for a saddle horse, and 2d. for a donkey. There were lots of donkeys grazing on the hills in those days'.

'Down on the road', she continued, 'was a small pub kept by a couple known as Mum and Dad. Everyone loved those two. Neither of 'em could read or write, so Dad always reckoned up the score with scratches on the wall. One day, when they were both dead and the pub gone, the road-mender noticed a ragged old man staring at the house, 'Who lives there now?' he asked.

When the road-mender told him, he said, 'Many's the drink I've had there. But tisn't for that I minds it best. 'Twas the warmth and the laughing and I don't know what'. And with that the poor old chap gave a great sigh and shuffled on.

'It was rare good drink too. Mum and Dad brewed it themselves in their own malt-house, and drew the water for it from a spring beside their door. The furnace used for the malting stands there now and catches water that folk still fetch, for there's none laid on here'.

Up the steep slippery slope above Mrs. Griffiths lived the roadman and his wife, an uncommonly good-looking pair, in a house built at the foot of an old quarry. The rock towers behind it and close under the rock was a sea-green pool, where orangetummied newts could be seen at the right season wriggling among the weeds. The wife told me that a rope-maker who once lived in their house used the quarry as a rope-walk, and laid his ropes out to dry in sun and wind on the terrace beside the pool. Once the Twitchen had its own John Silver.

'I remember when I was young', said old Chapman, 'there used to be three men with only three legs atween'em. Two had lost a leg in the Crimean War. I don't rightly know about the third. He had a terrible quick temper and when the children teased him he'd slip off his wooden leg in a flash and fling it straight at them. It was "see how they run" then, and serve them right too if one of them got hit'.

The more I talked to the people of the Twitchen the more I realised what a remarkably self-supporting little community it had been once. Not only did it possess its own Chapel, shop, pub, malthouse, toll-gate, rope-maker, herbalist, but also a cobbler who kept everyone well shod, and a tailor employing two apprentices. He lived on the hillside above the toll-gate.

'Such clothes he made. You couldna hardly wear 'em out in a lifetime', said the old man. 'One Christmas the tailor, after carol-singing and refreshments, grew too merry. So they shut him up in an outhouse at the Vicarage for the night, and let him out next morning when he had sobered down'.

Like so many hamlets, the Twitchen had dwindled in size. At least eight houses had disappeared, I was told. Fortunately, the old ones that remain are almost as solid as the hillside above them, and will stand for many a generation yet, while jerry-built bungalows come and go.

I hope nobody will doll-up the Twitchen too much. Such things do happen. And I hoped that Mr. Chapman would pass our gate for many a year before he measured his coffin-boards for the last time.

Kempton

North of the village the little river Kemp rises high up at Totterdown to join the Clun a mile away to the east. Beside it stands Kempton, a part of our parish, and there, in its wooded park, is Walcot, a handsome red-brick house, presented to Robert Clive by a nation, so grateful at first, so harsh in later judgments. Above it stretched a big wood with the word 'Plassy' fashioned by dark firs set among pale larches. This celebrated Clive's famous victory, and was planted by the Earl of Powis, his direct descendant, to celebrate the birth of his eldest son. The letters stood out clearly when we drove along the road to Bishops Castle.

But many things vanished during the Second World War, and 'Plassy' among them. This was deliberate destruction. Walcot Park harboured large ammunition dumps and the authorities feared their whereabouts might be given away by that outstanding word among the trees.

In our time the Park contained nothing more dangerous than a wonderful collection of water-fowl from all over the world. The long artificial lake was full of them, and the two brothers who now owned Walcot allowed us to watch them when we pleased. In particular I remember the little ducks who whistled in the trees, and a North American ruddy female pochard who relentlessly pursued an unwilling mandarin drake. Whenever he tried to escape she interposed her large body between him and the direction he wished to take, and so overwhelmed him with caresses that his plumage suffered grievously. There was also an old goose of such low mentality that when someone placed a stone across her path she continued to bump into it every time she went that way.

One day when we had been some time at Clunbury, the brothers invited us to meet a distinguished visitor, no less than Haile Selassie, exiled Emperor of Abyssinia, a small black-bearded man of compelling dignity. He spoke no English and unfortunately my hosts mistakenly credited me with fluent French, and placed me next to him—that is, in an armchair at least a couple of yards away. In spite of my intense admiration and sympathy for him and his country, I found it impossible to proclaim it across this horrid gap, especially as the other guests seemed to be sitting in dead silence. In desperation I told him how I and my family had raced toy-ducks down a mountain stream that morning. This to a man who had lived through terrible dangers and difficulties ever since he was a boy! He listened gravely and without comment and I'm sure thought I had entered my second childhood. Tom fared better. He accompanied a village table-tennis team to play the Walcot staff that evening. The Emperor came in to watch and chatted to him in friendly fashion. The royal party included Haile Selassie's daughter, widow of Ras Desta, recently beheaded by the Italians. I shall never forget the tragic look in her eyes. She did not try to talk to us. How could she?

While the Walcot estate still belonged to the Powis family they played an important part in the life of Kempton. The blacksmith's wife, a delightful woman with curly black hair, thick dark eyebrows and apple-red cheeks, told me about it.

In old Lord Powis' time Kempton was a much livelier place, she said. The majority of the village men worked on the estate and included gardeners, carpenters, cooper, brewer, game-keepers. The Head Forester ruled over thirty to forty woodmen. The Saw Yard alone employed twenty to thirty men—sawyers, carpenters, engine-driver, blacksmith and clerk of the works. Others worked at the dairy. The old Lord, a bachelor, came to the Hall for three months in the year with his two sisters. They drove about in a four-in-hand coach, with a postillion, dressed in scarlet, riding one of the front horses. Quite half the village always turned out to see them arrive. The women bobbed, the men touched their caps, but later enjoyed jokes about their landlord, though they respected and admired him. Many were the stories told of him.

'He got some strange ideas, that old Earl', said one man. 'Did his best to persuade a Clunbury man to sit for seven years in a hermit's cell in the Park and never to cut his hair or his beard'.

'I'll see to it you're comfortable down there. They'll feed you like a king and when you come out you won't lack for nothing', says the Earl.

'But William, he answered as he'd rather have his comforts now and above ground. So nothing ever came of it, though the Earl badgered him mightily'. But I never felt convinced that his suggestion was a serious one.

'In the days when folk used to build them a house between sunset and sunrise, and have a right to keep it provided they'd a fire burning in the chimney next morning, some of 'em got to work on the Powis foothills over Montgomery way. Then the Earl —a crafty old beggar he was—would send up one of his men with an offer to help and later stick the owner for some big sum and so rob him of his independence'.

Here, perhaps, his sense of property conquered his humanity. An example of this happened when, as he was walking round the village looking at one of the cottage gardens, a little girl said to him, 'My mum has a prettier one than that. Come and see it'. She took his hand and he went with her.

'Round Kempton there was much planting of foreign oaks, such as Italian and Turkish, in the last century', my informant told me. The wood was softer, disease was introduced, the acorns were not so good for the cattle and pigs. Nothing could beat English oaks. Old Earl Powis, he had cut down a terrible number in Walcot Park. This reminded him to tell me of an old man who worked there and noticed a tidy lot of bannets (walnuts) on a tree in a remote bit of the Park. 'So when dusk was falling he goes along and helps himself to a sackful. But as he carries them home who does he meet but the old Earl.'

'"Why, William, what you got there?" says the Earl.

'"Just a few bannets, nothen much", sez William, careless-like.

'"That's alright", sez the Earl, "you can leave 'em at the Hall as you go by". Course, William, he'd meant to take 'em to a very different place'.

But the old Earl could be generous too, and, as I have said, was generally popular. At Kempton Wakes, the first week in July, when the Foresters and Oddfellows marched round the village with banners flying, and a Robin Hood on horseback behind them, he produced a grand supply of cakes and cider. And when his eldest son came of age two 200 gallon casks of beer, made on the estate, were drunk in Kempton. Because of all this and the employment he created; the excitement of his arrival; the material for lively gossip he provided, the village was a sadder place when the estate was sold.

Kempton Wakes was the time when everyone began to dig their new potatoes. In those old days there was a woman who sold delicious home-made bread, and grew two or three pear trees in her garden. As soon as they ripened she made pear pies and gave them to all her customers.

Harry Mold, the blacksmith (known by another and more suitable title now) was a brother of our own smith at Clunbury. He, like his wife, was full of reminiscences of old days. One concerned a village cobbler who would set out to walk through the night to Shrewsbury, twenty-five miles away, to fetch fresh supplies of leather and return next day.

Then there was a one-armed drover named Ned who travelled

the sheep-walks right down to the south of England with a dog known far and wide for his clever ways.

When fresh from school Harry and his brothers drove the mail-run up the Clun Valley to Newcastle, delivering letters all the way along.

At Newcastle they built a little hut, from which they could do a bit of shooting, earn a few pence for odd jobs, and return with the out-going post in the afternoon. The pay was small but they were happy as kings. He had attended the village school, and a proper good school it was, with as many as a hundred children sometimes. A number walked as much as four miles. They were wonderful good children, and some of the boys sang in the choir and learned to ring the bells. Only once did he remember a proper rumpus. The boys loved to kick an old tin down the street—made a real game of it. But one day they did it on a Sunday. Out came the vicar in a roaring rage. 'Don't ever dare to do that again'. The boys fled.

Country Talk

One night Harry Meredith and his brother George came to supper and we had a long chat over the fire about people and places.

They knew their countryside as no outsider could ever hope to know it. Both were tolerant but held strong views about current social injustices. A keen sense of humour—Harry's more caustic, George's gentler—saved them from any bitterness.

Their bodies were typical of them, broad, solid, muscular, and so were their wide, good-humoured faces, Harry's a little shrewder and sterner, George's transparent and guileless as a child's with a smooth domed forehead and large innocent blue eyes. We talked of a host of things over mugs of Harry's home-brewed cider.

First of a Mr. Dyke, who once lived in our house—the one to which we moved later. He made his money by sheep farming and when he had laid up a tidy sum he migrated here from the Radnorshire hills. That, it seemed, was common custom hereabouts. You work desperately hard in a hard land and then drop down into Shropshire for a softer life. Mr. Dyke was an obstinate old man. When he worked in his garden he invariably threw his weeds, and loose stones as well, over the hedge on to the road, just as he

34

would have done on his Radnorshire farm. A neighbour grew furious and long and loud were the arguments.

'You could hear them all down the street', said Harry. 'Old Dyke would end by saying, "I always done it up at D—, and I'll do it here, say what you please!"—and then he'd fling an extra large weed over the wall'.

Fred o'Windy (Fred Davies was his proper name), now you ought to have known him. He lived up at Windy Corner above Obley and always wore a great moleskin coat. He poached in a grand way when he was young. One day a hen and her chickens were missing from someone's yard, and just such a brood was found up at Fred's. The policeman came to arrest him, marched him off and shut him in a cell, and put the hen and her brood safely in a shed. But next morning she and her chicks had clean disappeared. One of his pals had let them out. So for lack of evidence the case was dropped. This seemed peculiar to us.

'A knowing land-owner took Fred for his keeper later, and a proper one he made. Up to all the tricks was Fred. The other poachers knew their time was up when he began lording it about with a gun in his hand.

'Young George Owen (brother he was to the gardener at the Vicarage, what used to watch us from the belfry when we worked as lads under him) had the snaring rights on a bit of land up at the Llan. One day a pal noticed another man a-creeping along in the dusk setting his wires up there. "Ha, ha", thinks he, "you're hoping to help yourself to George's rabbits, are you?"

'So he gets up very early next morning, takes all the rabbits from the wires, and when he comes to the last he writes on a bit of paper, "Good morning, George" ('this other poacher, he was called George too'),

"I got all your rabbits, of that there is no doubt,
    And 'tis a thousand chances you'll ever find me out".
Then away he went with the rabbits, pleased with the first bit of poetry he ever wrote'.

'I'd ha given something to see t'other chap's face when he read it', added Harry.

'Old Doctor Brown—he what was doctor here when we was boys—he couldna abear the church bells. He was a terrible hard drinker and when he'd got the delirium tremens and one of us was a-sitting with him, he'd keep saying sarcastic-like, "Ain't them bells lovely, ain't them bells sweet? Ding-dong, ding-dong, till your head's fit to burst!" Mrs. Brown, she came as the first nurse ever they had round here. She gave out to be Church of England and went to church reg'lar, but as soon as she'd married the doctor, bless me if she didn't blossom out into a full-fledged Roman Catholic!'

Harry Mold had also talked of Dr. Brown, 'Not a bad old chap but terrible fond of drink. He travelled by pony and trap for miles along the bad roads, and a young lad looked after the pony and stayed beside it when the doctor was visiting a patient'.

He'd been on the job himself for a while, and found the waiting about terrible tedious. It was not only the visits. The lad in charge—if not himself, then one of his family—was bidden to be round with the trap at 10 a.m. but just about then the doctor would take a book to the privy in the garden, and a mug of beer, and then sit for half-an-hour, while boy and pony chafed outside.

Always the doctor's round took him past the Hundred House where a great stone jar that he always carried would be filled up with beer, and maybe he would stop to listen to a bit of singing. The Hundred House used to be a lively place, and, like other pubs, was open all day. Farm labourers and other workmen sometimes spent two whole days inside. They could buy ample bread and cheese for twopence, tobacco cost only threepence an ounce, and a pint of beer threepence. Their bosses knew where to find them, but since they never had a proper holiday nothing was said. Very nice voices the men had, and after a drink they felt courage to get on their feet.

'There was a Dick Luscott from Clunton Coppice, as lost his way in the woods on his way home after a merry evening at the Hundred House. An owl was calling, 'Who, Who' and Dick shouted, "Tis Dick Luscott from the Coppice'. Again the owl said 'Who, Who?' and again Dick shouted back. After the third time he told the owl, 'Come and see for yourself, Owd bird!'

I have an idea the story is told of other night revellers, but this was the local version.

When Dr. Brown was disposed of George and Harry told us of places to visit.

'The Rock o'Woolbury above Clun—that's a grand great quarry. So big you could put the village inside it. They say all the stone for Clun Castle came from there. The big rock at the far end is called the Pulpit Rock. There's a deep cleft near by, and when you drop a stone into it you can hear it going down, down, down. They say there's an underground passage there all the way to the castle. Above the quarry is a rock called the Devil's Armchair and bless me, if it isn't just like a chair. You can sit yourself down and look all around the hills'.

Sheep

Our valley was always alive from end to end with sheep, most of them true natives; the black-faced Clun Valley breed. But the larger, longer-woolled, white-faced Kerries also abounded, and a fair sprinkling, on the higher ground, of agile little Welsh sheep. Because the Cluns were the favourite, tales were told of how sometimes a white-faced sheep had her face black-leaded in order to include her with Clun sheep at sale time. Once for a sale in aid of Chapel funds, someone played this trick.

'A young fellow who would only have black-faced sheep in his flock bought this Kerry', a farmer's wife told me. 'That night it rained in torrents, so by morning all the black had been washed away—and wasn't he in a towering rage!'

She admitted that once she had done much the same herself.

'One of our Clun sheep had only a small black mark on its nose, and Dad was proper vexed and said, "That one looks a bit of a cross-bred". So I blacked its face all over for the Craven Arms Sheep Sale'.

Just before this all-important event I found her scrubbing the faces of the Kerries to smarten them up, while the farm boy held their heads. Otherwise her task would have been hopeless for they showed their resentment by stamping and struggling. Great value, inspired by a purely aesthetic motive, attached to the dyeing of the sheep for Craven Arms, and Kerry September sales. They must look their best on these occasions, and gay colours attracted the eye.

At this time of year it was a pleasure to wander in the fields and see how all the flocks had blossomed into primrose, buttercup, orange, deep pink, or Japonica red. Different shades were considered right, if not essential, for different breeds. Kerries sported coats of yellow-ochre; for the Clun Valleys 'Sunrise' was favoured.

One year I remarked that the sheep at the farm where my friend lived had changed to an unusually dark red.

'Yes', she answered, 'Dad was proper put out about that. He told me to get some Venetian Red in Craven Arms, and so I did. But they should have mixed something else in with it'.

I remember, how, before I had grown accustomed to all this burst of colour in late summer, just outside Craven Arms I saw from a little distance what I took for a number of gigantic vegetable marrows lying under a hedge. Then, to my astonishment, one of them got up and began to walk. The flock had been driven a long way for the Sale, and had lain down to rest.

Clearly the sheep themselves hated this 'dolling up', for as I roamed about I found how hard they had tried to rid themselves of the powder clinging to their coats. Gates, palings, tree trunks were often deep orange or red.

One evening as we returned from an expedition in the Teme Valley, I saw something that carried me straight back to 'The Return of the Native'. Long shadows, stealing down the hillside, threw into brilliant relief a flock of golden sheep. A young man strode towards them. His bare arms, his hair, his shirt matched the colour of his flock. He was a strangely glowing figure in the low sunlight— an earthy figure, yet one who seemed to belong to another world; the world of Samuel Palmer. Because I had grown up in Wiltshire, where the sheep-fold, hurdled round and lined with straw, played so important a part in January and February—the folds to which the shepherd led his flock on winter evenings—because of this I was amazed to see how casually these Shropshire sheep dropped their lambs all over the fields; sometimes in the shelter of a hedge, but often far out in the open. Most of them survived, though now and then, when the flock was big and scattered, one found a little dead body lying in the grass.

Once, at an upland farm, I came on a small girl solemnly planting a Union Jack mounted on a stick into the ground beside a tiny feeble lamb. Was she expecting its death and setting up a memorial? No, she said, it was to scare away the crows while she went into the house for her dinner. There were some very wicked crows about but, she asserted, 'they couldna abear that flag'. She was not more than seven years old, but so serious, so dedicated.

We woke in the mornings in early spring to a chorus of lambs, and wherever we went little black faces peered through the hedges, or agile bodies, which had squeezed their way out, bounded before us down the lane. Sometimes, round an old tree-stump, the lambs were playing a game of 'I'm the King of the Castle', to Jill's delight. These were the healthy ones without a care in the world—who, with a wag of their tails could leap straight into the air with no preliminary run. A small minority survived with difficulty and prolonged bottle-feeding.

One evening as I returned from visiting patients with Tom we met a farmer and his wife, driving some sheep and lambs before them, and each of them carried a lamb. Further on we passed the home of our District Nurse, there she was cradling another as tenderly as a human baby.

I well remember my first tiddling. Bleating piteously, he struggled to catch up with a sheep who pursued her stolid way and completely ignored him. The poor little creature was badly hampered by the skin of a dead lamb tied round his neck. It trailed behind him so that he seemed like a child in too long a frock. I wanted to help him but thought I might only harm his cause if I picked him up and plumped him beside the mother. Perhaps in the end he would melt her heart and waken her maternal instincts by sheer persistence.

In a certain upland field, an old farmer, busy among his flock, told me how hard life could be in lambing time when a man did all his own work. Rain had set in that year just as it began, and he reckoned it had fallen almost continually for nine whole days. Sometimes the wind changed four times in a night, and that meant shifting the sheep from one hedge to another. Many lambs and ewes too, had died that Spring.

'Pray the Lord the worst be over now', he said.

He spoke of his difficulty in getting young sheep to feed their babies, like young gad-about wives who hated to give up their usual outings. 'When this happens, I ties my dog to a bush, and the sheep, who always feels him her enemy, thinks, "Aha!! Now I can master him and get my own back!" So she starts a threatening and abutting at him. Then I creeps up with the lamb, and it draws a morsel of milk before she knows what's happening. After that she canna spurn the little creature any more'.

'Ah', he continued after a pause, 'sheep bring a lot of worry. Soon I'll have to go out at evening to make sure no lambs have struck'. This was a new word to me.

'Means they've been frolicking about and over-heated theirselves, then laid down, got chilled, and gone all stiff. When that
happens they wunna recover unless you catch 'em in time and
snip their tails. 'Tis the shock does it, I reckon'.

No sooner in late May or early June did the weather turn
kind and warm than sheep-washing started all down the valley.
While still in bed early one perfect morning I heard the sheep
passing down the street to the Brook. I hurried out and found
the old farmer and his lad busy near the bridge, in the shadow of
the poplar trees; the penned-up flock behind them were in shadow
too, and the pool beside them. Beyond the shadow was the flashing
silver river and the sunlit meadow, where the newly-washed were
feeding placidly with their families, their own troubles over.

But from the pen came lugubrious noises as the remainder waited
their turn. I watched the whole process carefully. The boy would
open the hurdle, seize the nearest sheep, drag her to the water's
edge, and turn her with a dextrous twist on her side. Then he held
her in position while he and his master trimmed the matted wool
round her tail and looked for ticks. After this they slipped a noose
round her neck, thrust a hook through it, and plop into the Brook
she went. Each time she tried to rise the boy mercilessly thrust
her down with his plunger, and kept her under (all but her head)
for some thirty seconds raking her back the while. Now and then
the victim baaed piteously, but as a rule accepted her fate in stoic
silence. From under a hawthorn-tree on the bank the lambs stared
anxiously, wondering what appalling fate had overtaken their
mothers. Washing well and truly done, the farmer neatly slipped the
noose from the sheep's neck, and she climbed heavily out, her coat
so sodden that at first she could barely stand. Once on top of the
bank she would pause a moment, while a thousand rivulets streamed
from her. Her lamb, or perhaps two lambs, ran to her to sniff her
curiously. Could this waterfall truly be their mother? At first
she seemed too abject to heed them, but in a few minutes there she
was in the sunlit meadow cropping busily, her children at her side,
her ordeal forgotten. Hilda Gittoes, a shepherd's daughter, told me
that the newly-married, town-bred, wife of a local farmer, hearing
that the sheep were to be washed that day, asked how much soap
she ought to provide. That remained a good joke for a long
while.

When shearing started the whole valley echoed with the cries of the sheep, and once as I walked above Clun on a wild windy day a mass of wool came blowing down the road.

A black sheep sometimes appeared in a flock, and an old friend in the village told how her father always kept one so that her mother might knit him the striped black and white stockings that he liked to wear.

Village Broadcasts

During our first experience of floods I was told a tragic tale. A young man, trying at night to cross the river by a foot-bridge that had just been swept away, was drowned in the dark torrent. His story lingered in my mind and ended in a play with this tragedy as climax.

My young man, sick to death of life on a tyrannical father's farm, resolves to seek work in the town. Mother and sister plead with him in vain. Between him and his father a bitter quarrel breaks out, and the father, in a raging temper, turns him straight into the stormy night, with a 'Go to the Devil!' He watches the boy plunge into the darkness, and hears a terrible cry as he stands in the doorway.

I got together, easily enough, a little band of players and we produced the play at a local Drama Festival with no very brilliant result. Foolishly I had personified the spirits of the river and the hill to dissuade the young man from his purpose as he sits brooding by the fire. But in spite of its defects my company seemed to like the play, and, greatly daring, I sent it to the Midland B.B.C. at Birmingham. To my surprise it was accepted. *But,* came the edict, those misconceived spirits must go. I hurried up to my attic and cut them out immediately. Now came a charming person called Charles Brewer to meet my company. At his request I offered alternative actors for the principle parts. One was the porter at the local station. Because he could not leave his post Charles Brewer listened to him read his part in the waiting-room, and chose him for the young man. After careful rehearsal we set off to act our play in the Birmingham studio. All went well. The only hostile criticism came from a farmer's wife who declared, apropos of the father's language, 'Shropshire farmers never swear'. 'My word!' commented a neighbour, 'she should hear her husband on market days!'

Not long afterwards two young B.B.C. men arrived to ask if I would arrange a broadcast, wherein a number of people would each speak of some particular aspect of their life, and so offer as complete a picture as possible of the village.

Soon I had seven grown-ups and two children sitting round a good log fire in the evenings talking freely, while I scribbled frantically. The adults drank home-made cider, the children ginger-beer. Our schoolmaster spoke of fishing and of floods. Our builder of poaching in the Brook in his young days. Harry of cider-making and the church-bells. Hilda of whinberry-picking. An old farm labourer of the work when he was young, and a young one of how things were today. The children chattered of what the Brook meant to them—of their paddling, their fishing, their feasts of 'crab' at the water's edge. Old Mr. Chapman from the Twitchen agreed at first to take part, but later, returning from the accustomed inspection of his coffin-boards, he looked in to say that he felt too old.

Our broadcast ended with the elder farm labourer singing in his high-pitched voice, 'Brigham Young', a song he had sung at Penny-Readings sixty years before, when the Mormons were much in the news. We all listened with delight, especially when he sang the last verse, about the faithless wife, with gusto—

'If she is in a railway train I hope that he will smash,
If up in a balloon, she fall out with a crash.
If on the road to Salt Lake I hope that she be drowned,
And I will get another, and quickly will be bound'.

Then all joined in the chorus:
'P'raps she's on the railway
With a swell so fair,
P'raps she's up in a balloon,
A flying through the air,
P'raps she's dead, p'raps alive,
P'raps she's on the sea,
P'raps she's gone to Brigham Young
A Mormonite to be'.

We repeated these fireside gatherings many times and the stream of reminiscences never failed. Undoubtedly everybody enjoyed themselves, I as much as anyone. Indeed, I learned more about the village in those weeks than I had in three years. Much of the talk is already embodied in other sections of this book but here are a few odd items.

42

Harry, his broad face shining in the firelight as he sipped his cider, spoke of the cider-press that still came round each autumn. He reckoned that seven or eight hogshead were made in the last year, as compared with at least forty in the days when an old stone press was used. But that was a slow job.

He told of a barrel of cider without a lid, and a layer of chaff spread over the top of the scum to keep it air-tight. Soon one of the farm cats disappeared, then another, then another. Everyone said what a good flavour that cider had—'only mebbe it was a bit sharp-like, and reason why, the skeletons of all those cats were found later in the bottom of one barrel!'

My team were very proud of a local horse, The Colonel, who won The Grand National two years in succession. The odds were fifty to one against him when he first ran, but some local folk were in the know, and a butler up at the Hall made £400 and set himself up in a pub. Another local celebrity was Mr. Cooper, of sheep-dip fame.

'Corn', said the young labourer, 'was still ground on a few out-of-the-way farms with a "Jenny-ring", but 'tis a ticklish business if the horse turns fidgety'.

As for sheep he and all the men agreed there were none to beat the Clun Forests. For one thing they stuck to their own pasture better than the little Welsh sheep, so there was less 'glutting' (filling in gaps in the hedges) to be done.

The children were a joy to listen to because of their complete lack of self-consciousness. At the end of all this talk I gave each member of the team a copy of their part, put into their own words and with freedom to alter anything they wished. Rehearsals began in earnest and finally the two young men came again to supervise our final one.

At last we were ready to set off, in three cars, for Birmingham, and when our broadcast was over we celebrated it with a good supper before we started back. Then bad luck hit us. When I and my contingent were still twenty-four miles from home my head-lights failed. It was now midnight, and no garage open, nor even one on our road. I must drive at a snail's-pace, while Hilda and the children slept peacefully. But Harry stayed wide awake to keep me company.

As the day of the broadcast approached various reporters had wandered round the village, including one who took really beautiful photographs. Finally, on the eve of our journey to Birmingham, two young men arrived to interview me. I had just finished washing Jill's hair, and she was drying it beside the fire in her long white night-dress.

'Now, what a pretty picture she'd make sitting in front of your wireless', said one, 'we would call it "Listening to Mummy's Broadcast".' I told them politely but firmly they could do no such thing. As a doctor's wife I would certainly not give the impression that at five years old she stayed up at night listening to the wireless.

Perhaps I may be forgiven for quoting our best Press notice. The *Manchester Guardian* wrote:

'Of its own kind this broadcast was perfect, and one of the most pleasing things we have ever heard. The village people . . . talked, described their work, sang a few songs, and seemed entirely unselfconscious. The simplicity, almost the poetry of their speech, the soft border accents, were all alike delightful'.

Our people were enchanted by their brief fame, by the photographs, by the recognition they received when they went to Shrewsbury. Then the village settled back into its usual quiet life.

Our final effort was a play for Children's Hour about witchcraft in Shropshire in old days. It was broadcast to 'The Empire' as well as on the Home Service, which sounded very grand.

As I started off with some of my cast a glance behind showed me that two of the children had daubed their mouths with scarlet lipstick.

'Oh', I said, 'the B.B.C. are expecting two nice little country girls'.

There was some whispering and giggling. When I looked round their mouths looked natural again.

IV

BESIDE THE BROOK

That first evening ramble beside the Brook was the forerunner of many, at all times of day, at all seasons. Some I remember more vividly because of their link with a particular event. Such was my first encounter with a curlew. Though snow still ribbed the hills, Spring was in the air as I set off upstream one day in early March. The water was a deep blue-green. A kingfisher, perched on a tree stump, repeated this colour in a heightened, shining fashion. The sheep feeding on the banks carried the blue of the sky on their backs. Alder-catkins powdered with crimson dust swayed above the surface.

I had noted all these, and then, lost in thought, was startled by a delicious bubbling high overhead, half call, half song. It reminded me for an instant of a gigantic nightingale, so strange, so beautiful, that I thought I must be dreaming. But soon the sound floated down again, and a large, long-billed bird shot from the sky and skimmed over the grass. Then I realised, from a picture in my bird book, that I had seen a curlew, the first of many hundreds. That ecstatic bubbling thrills me afresh every time, but never with the intensity of my first experience. Some people, like a woman living under the Long Mynd, find it gloomy and saddening. 'That miserable old bird—it gives me the creeps', she said. But for me it expressed a rapture that no other bird can equal. Spring, eternal Spring was in it, and the whole freedom of the sky.

When there was no time for a leisurely ramble, I would sit on the bank just beyond the orchard for a few minutes with a book. Once, looking up suddenly, I saw a kingfisher on a low hanging bough only three yards away. There he stayed for several minutes, gently bowing his enchanting body. The irridescence of his back, his chestnut throat, made a sight to revel in. I pretended to be buried in my book, but stole frequent glances. He soon flew away, but when I next looked up *three* kingfishers sat on the bough, father, mother and young one. Their vivid, shiny beauty stayed with me all day.

Sometimes a dull job in the kitchen was transformed by the glimpse from the window of a kingfisher flashing past.

For three months after our arrival the Brook remained comparatively peaceful, but one night towards the end of May, we were wakened by a terrific thunderstorm, followed by the lash of rain against the window and a roar of water. Daylight revealed our gentle Brook as a surging chocolate flood. Unused to its ways, the change we found almost unbelievable. It was bearing along a mass of driftwood, composed, so it seemed, of black monsters, distorted limbs, and writhing fish-like forms. Quivering creamy foam filled every little bay.

The rain fell all that day and all the next night till the Brook was actually washing over the foot-bridge to Chapel Farm, and came creeping up the steps to our yard. Just before sunset it ceased and a little knot of villagers gathered there to chat about former floods.

'Eh', said one old inhabitant, 'but this binn nothing to a May flood back in 1885. First there was an almighty fall of snow, and then it rained seventy hour wi'out a stop. The whole valley was one great lake'.

In 1910 there was another severe flood, when a man was marooned in his cottage in the meadow under Clunton Coppice for three days with his pig. He hung a sheet from the bedroom window to show that he was safe and sound, and that no one need worry about him.

I asked if he was still alive.

'Oh ah', answered the old man. 'George Chester be at the Trinity Hospital up at Clun now'.

This I knew to be the name of the old almshouses, and I promised myself that I would hear the story at first-hand one day. Now the schoolmaster arrived to tell of a cloud-burst in the hills above the source of the Brook in 1927 that set it in full flood. Within a couple of hours, because the hay harvest was late that year, tons of hay were afloat till, by evening, the whole river was blocked. Higher up, cider casks laid on the banks to dry, went bobbing along to the next village, and the folk there caught them and began to trundle them home, when up galloped the owners in their carts, shouting and gesticulating to claim their property. The cloggers suffered too.

They had been busy among the alders close to the village and had left a great stack of clogs piled on the banks. Soon these were all swirling and dancing on the current.

'And the rabbits!' joined in a young man. 'They'd been driven from their burrows, and to save themselves they climbed into the trees and hedges. But us boys waded in with sticks and there were not many rabbits left at the end'.

'One comical thing I do mind', said the old inhabitant. 'A hen was brooding her eggs on top of a truss of hay, and I'm blessed if the fond old bird didna sit tight on her nest till they took her off, nest and all, a few miles downstream'.

This flood of ours was the first of many. They did little harm, brought down good red sandstone, and never failed to excite and delight me. But before I say more of them I must tell of a visit I paid to the man, very old now, at Trinity Hospital, built for twelve old men in the early seventeenth century. I waited to hear the story of his confinement with his pig from his own lips. He was crouching over the fire in the big store room, looking like a dilapidated clergyman in the queer rusty black garment, half coat and half cloak, worn by the pensioners. His battered clerical hat was pulled well down on his head, and the smoke of the fire was drifting about the room and up to the high stone ceiling. He seemed pleased to tell his tale.

'"Lord a mercy, whatever be up?" I sez to mesself when I heard a lot o' ole jam jars tinkling round me house. Why, 'tis Noah's flood all over again, I sez, when I seed all that water and all that darkness in the sky. So I runs down in my nightshirt and fetches my owd pig in from the sty. She took a lot of pushing and pricking to get her up the stairs, but I wanna gwaine to lose her, flood or no flood. When I'd got 'er safe into my bedroom, I runs down and fetches every morsel of food I could lay hands on, and all the while the water creeping in till the chairs was afloat. For three whole days I and my old pig bided up there. Proper company she was, and 'twas a long time after afore I could abear to kill her. When the water went down', he went on, staring into the fire as though he saw it all again, 'it left a pretty how d'ye do—wood lying thick on the brick floor and that as wet as the river-bed. But I'd stacked some dry sticks upstairs and soon had a fire burning. So there I sat with me feet on a bundle of old sacks to keep 'em out of the damp. And when I'd dried some of the driftwood I had a blaze fit to warm a king, and I didna mind a morsel about the flood—not a morsel, I didna'.

He stirred up the fire, and sat smiling into it.

The memory of his sojourn with his pig was clearly a landmark in his life.

The Coracle

That first flood settled one thing. We must have a small boat of some kind, to take us not only on the Brook, but across wide flooded fields. Someone suggested a coracle as the answer; fishermen used them on the Severn at Shrewsbury. So a patient of Tom's made one for us—a round tub-like affair of ash-lathes covered with tarred canvas. It gave us immense joy, but experience taught us to use it with great caution. The boys gradually learned to manoeuvre it rightly after they had spun round in vain circles on the Weir Pool many times. Not till the next flood did I venture in it myself to remain there only a few seconds. Oliver, the wretch, pushed me off too hard. Over went the coracle leaving me in ice-cold water. I ran home with a single thought. A hot bath! But, oh misery, the Triplex had gone out and there was not a drop of hot water to be had. I vowed after this to master this treacherous craft for myself without help from my sons, and so was able when the next flood came to enjoy it to the full.

After twenty-four hours of continuous rain I woke to hear it still streaming against our windows with slightly guilty joy. The brook would be up again, the fields flooded. The non-arrival of our milk at breakfast strengthened this belief. Water was again washing over the foot-bridge. At the earliest possible moment Jill, now five years old, and I wheeled the coracle on a barrow to the meadow below the bridge. The rain had stopped and the world looked enchanting; the hills the colour of bunched violets, the woods wine-red above sheets of shining water. The wind, warm and kind, roared triumphantly through the poplar trees. We paddled our craft in all directions, using every current except one that would have swept us straight into the foaming racing brown river. To speak of it as a brook at such times would be wholly inappropriate. A flock of ducks were enjoying themselves as much as we. Sometimes they dabbled in the shallow water, sometimes, growing bolder, they plunged into the current and with loud rapturous quacks let themselves be swept downstream. Then, collecting into a dense body, and flapping their wings to clear them of water, they beat their way back to safety. Only the sheep looked unhappy. They stood about on little islands of grass, and watched us with melancholy yellow eyes.

Presently Tom came down to see what was happening, and when we told him we longed to navigate that particularly swift current but dare not for fear of being carried away, the noble fellow fetched his fishing waders and placed himself ready to stop our headlong course before we passed danger point.

At last, after several thrilling voyages, the coracle capsized and I fell into the water with Jill on top of me. She was merely a little splashed but I was soaked to the skin. Still, this time it had been worth it.

We lived through many a flood after that. As I think of them a whole reel of pictures unwinds before me. Of days when there was no colour anywhere, when a blanket of clouds lay low over the hills, and the grey stretches of water were bounded by jet-black hedges and trees. Of days when the whole world seemed on the move, with trees bending; flood water sweeping the fields and breaking into tiny waves; peewits swirling, clouds racing; only the dark hills motionless. Pictures of moonlight nights when you looked across a sheet of silver that held fast in the waters a ball of pale gold. Once, on such a night, I came on a flock of geese sporting themselves in the shallows, their bodies startlingly white against the darker glitter behind them.

But of course floods played only a small part in the pageant of the year.

Frost

There were the frosty days that turned the Brook into Fairyland.

One day when it seemed as if the east wind would blow forever, when the ground was hard as iron, and snowdrops lay prostrate in the garden, it was gorgeous by the Brook. Never had I seen such icicles. They floated along on bits of driftwood, they hung from the grass and rushes and the low drooping boughs. Where twigs touched the surface they had put on a coating of ice like little ballet skirts. Some were sets of glittering white teeth; some, jewels; some, delicate as lace handkerchiefs; some, tiny bells that tinkled as they knocked together in the wind. A heron, sitting motionless by the Weir Pool, looked as if he too were made of ice. All the small bays were frozen over and the Brook deep dark green, strangely still as though he too might freeze soon. And, day after day the wind went on blowing from the east, and the icicles grew larger each day and tinkled more clearly.

Spring and Summer

There were the Spring days when curlews returned to the water-meadows; when the dippers built on a mossy stump just beyond the orchard; when Tom started fishing again, and often brought two or three small trout proudly in to be cooked for supper. At times my heart grieved for him when, on his half-day, I had to hurry to the river bank with a belated call. I can still see the look on his expressive face, and hear the rarely uttered, but heartfelt 'Damn!'

And now lambs began to appear in the fields, lying in the open or sheltering in the lee of a hedge; never gathered into tidy folds like our Wiltshire sheep. And the summer days! They of course were best of all. The big field adjoining us went down to grass and to flowers. I've never known more flowery, more sweetly smelling grass. Moon-daisies, buttercups, red sorrel, yellow rattle, lousewort, ragged robin, clover, hawkweed, eyebright and many another. The eyebright, with its delicately curved face, and golden eye fringed with violet lashes, has always been a special favourite of mine, I remember my delight when I learned from my flower book that its other name, Euphrasia, means 'joy'.

Beside the Brook it grew luxuriantly. Harry described how, as children, he and his brothers would pick a great bunch for an old lady who lived at the little grey cottage under the Hill called Tansy Cottage and believed that an infusion of eyebright would make her eyes young again. She rewarded the boys with slices of bread thickly spread with blackcurrant jam.

I feel sadly afraid that should I go back now to the big field— the Hollytree Cow Pasture—I should no longer find that wealth of flowers, that fragrance, that hum of bees from the Mac's orchard, that used to delight me.

Summer was hey-day for the village children. They adored the Brook, and out of school hours there were usually a few playing on the little gravel beaches, or wading in the shallows in their gumboots. This, said the old folks, they too had always done, but because they had no gumboots in their young days, they waded in the water in their leather ones. Then they would go home and keep them on till bedtime, because if they told their mothers a walloping awaited them. In this way they firmly believed they had laid up for themselves a legacy of rheumatism.

One evening during that first summer I found six children crouched round a small fire cooking something in an old tin. 'What?' I asked.

'Crabs', answered the eldest, a girl named Olive, one of a family of ten who lived beside the Brook. I peered into the tin and saw a number of small crayfish. 'You won't over-eat yourselves', I said.

'There's always a nice bit in the tails', they told me. 'We get our crabs out of holes in the bank and under stones, you have to look out 'cos they nip your fingers *and* your toes'. What other fish did they catch? 'Bull-heads, short and fat with big heads', answered the children. 'And Davey loachers, long thin fish with whiskers. They'll nip you too if you gives 'em a chance'.

I begged them to be careful when fishing because of deep places in the river bed. They nodded their heads. 'We know all about *them*', said Olive. 'A little boy who'd gone bathing by himself was drowned in a hole near our cottage'.

On warm summer days we bathed in the Weir Pool, half-a-mile upstream, and carried picnic teas there. Once we took with us our vicar's wife, a round, sweet-tempered little woman. After one of the boys had given her a successful voyage in the coracle, she asked if she might go alone. But Oliver, again the villain, gave her too hard a push—not, I am sure from any malice or mischief, but from sheer exuberance. Over went the coracle, and there was our guest completely submerged. Oliver, deeply contrite, pulled her out and rescued her large hat, afloat in the middle of the pool. She behaved perfectly, no word of remonstrance, no crossness. Away she trotted to put on some dry clothes, showering little waterfalls behind her as she ran.

In a spell of high summer the boys decided to make use of a second coracle given them by a friend, and to go for a two-day excursion down the Brook. This coracle, though ancient, appeared watertight. They hoped to reach Leintwardine at the junction of the Brook with the Teme, where they would stay the night and continue their journey next day. Pyjamas were rolled in a water-proof bag, and Thomas carried a pound note in his pocket. They would telephone to us in the evening. To all this we agreed, with strict injunctions that on no account must they enter Downton Gorge, with its rocks and perils. When the right time came I would fetch them home, since coracles cannot be expected to fight against the current.

No one starting to cross the Atlantic in a small boat could have looked more serious and dedicated than they as they launched the two coracles just below the bridge, and disappeared under a tangle of trees.

About three hours later, as I sunned myself in peaceful solitude (Jill was away) and thought how pleasant to have lively children, but also how pleasant their absence sometimes is, two dejected boys appeared. They had carried one coracle home; the other had sprung a leak and lay at the bottom of the river. They'd tried in vain to pull it out. Might Harry help them tomorrow? It was all frightfully sad. But after hot baths and a good tea their spirits were high as ever.

Poaching

Other people went fishing in the Brook besides the children and the regular fishermen. When we came to the village I don't fancy much poaching took place, but earlier in the century it was going strong. I loved to hear our respectable builder-cum-church-warden tell how on moonlit Saturday nights, he and his gang had a fine time. Scarcely a cottage but had a trout sizzling in the pan on Sunday morning.

All sorts of people took part, including a butcher, a carpenter, a schoolmaster who spent his holidays in the village, and a tall man from a cottage in the meadows. 'Long Tom' they called him, and he was a rare one to poke the net in all the holes.

But once, I was told, a man went out alone—a daft thing to do—got tangled in his own net and drowned, poor chap.

Doubtless the godly quoted an appropriate verse from the Psalms, but so long as the inhabitants of a riverside village have no fishing rights many will consider poaching a most legitimate sport.

Otters

To see an otter—that became one of my dearest ambitions, now that a river flowed past my very door. Tom watched one as he fished in a pool beyond Clun, and another time two raced round the field quite close to him. A man who lived in a cottage by the Brook, went down with his pail to draw water one evening and there among the nettles sat a mother and her cubs. When she saw him she came at him. He dropped his pail and ran off as fast as his heels would carry him.

Yet though I set out night after night, trod with immense caution, fell over prostrate cows in the dark, and nearly landed myself in the Brook more than once, not a glimpse of an otter rewarded me. In desperation I chose a thundery evening because someone declared that was the best time. Not a breath stirred the trees; not a bird or beast moved. Then from the south came short quick reports, more like guns than thunder. But they sounded a long way off; I would not turn home yet. When I reached a cottage beside the Brook in the eastern meadows, my hopes rose high. Only half-an-hour ago the woman there had seen a baby otter, no bigger than a rabbit, she told me, swim upstream.

'Bide here a moment and maybe he'll be back again', she said. Grim clouds gathered on top of the hill; it grew so dark we could barely see each other's faces. The short reports turned into one huge roar as of a beast rolling down the hill and let loose in our valley. I fled, but was wet to the skin before I reached home. Once more I was a defeated and disappointed woman.

Downstream the Brook ran past the big farm, under a row of black poplars, whose leaves glittered like little gold platters in the Spring, and under arching alders and willows. It flowed on past Shepherd's Bridge, which the sheep crossed for washing and shearing, and continued its quiet way to Beambridge and a small group of cottages, where lived a railway porter, Don Davies, owner of a rich tenor voice and remarkable acting powers. Through a few more meadows, and it passed Coston Manor, where a strong-minded, warm-hearted Yorkshire woman, with six marmalade cats, gave us wonderful teas and let us bathe in her pool. In an old Chapel, now part of the farm out-buildings, two men, who had killed another in a fight, sought sanctuary.

More sheep; more Herefordshire cattle with their wide, white faces; more scattered farms; a beautiful old mill called Beckjay; more rapids and small pools, till finally our Brook was swallowed up by the wider, if, for us at all events, less loveable Teme. A journey upstream from our village was far longer and more eventful. The valley widens, then narrows again. Wooded hills on either side

David Jones

CLUN CASTLE

steepen, till the Brook reaches its metropolis, Clun. Here its importance seemed suddenly enhanced as it swept round three sides of the Castle.

Of my three special Castles, none stands so spectacularly. The ruined 12th century tower rears up on a high mound above the river with grim determination as though it was saying, 'Here I've stood for close on a thousand years, and here I'll stand yet another thousand', and indeed, when Llewelyn savaged the countryside and even burnt the town of Clun, the Castle defied him.

I loved to dawdle along the top of the moat, where sheep and lambs grazed, and to look down at the flashing, lively stream.

Though the Castle is the crown of Clun, Trinity Hospital is a beautiful, peaceful place too.

The stories of the men, who came here to rest as their lives drew to a close, for over 300 years, would make a fascinating chronicle could it ever be written. These pensioners had practiced a great variety of skills, including that of a clogger. Daily they filed into the old pews in the Chapel, and on Sundays and Saints' Days a good dinner with the Warden rewarded them. Kindly women cared for their needs, and restrictions were few. But for certain offences—principally drunkenness—a fine was exacted. These fines increased in severity each time the offence was repeated, and after the seventh, the culprit was 'gated' for a given period. If he again transgressed, he could be turned out and lose his little home and garden.

It seems that towards the end of the 19th century a lax and dishonest warden held office. He took the fines for his own use, and instead of either gating or discharging a culprit, he merely increased the fine—to his great personal advantage. After a while the Trustees discovered his true character and dismissed him.

His successor soon found out that one old man in particular had got drunk continually, far, far beyond seven times. A severe warning was given that should it happen again dismissal would inevitably follow. Once more he came reeling back to the Hospital, whereupon the Warden, the Vicar of Clun and the Trustees, and Lord Powis, Lord of the Manor of Clun, decreed that he must go. But nearly the whole population of Clun rose in his defence. They had grown fond of this old sinner and thought he should be allowed to end his days in peace. During the heated controversy over his fate an historical event saved him. Mafeking was relieved. Amid the delirious rejoicings that enlivened the whole of England he was reprieved, and lived on at the Hospital till he died. Whether he continued to get drunk history does not record.

I always found the Hospital garden, full of wallflowers, tulips, forget-me-nots, pansies, and surrounded by the old gabled houses, a rewarding place to wander in. No sooner did you pass through the heavy oak, nail-studded door, dated 1614, and see the old men sitting in the sunshine, than you seemed to share their peace. No doubt, like all of us, they were sinners in one way or another, but through their long lives they had laboured hard for a meagre wage, and now could live in comfort, if not luxury. My visit to old George Chester, crouching over his smoky fire, in his big cold room taught me that.

Many things have changed since those days. The rooms have been modernised, the ceilings lowered, a bathroom and lavatory installed in each cottage, and—perhaps most important of all— women live here as well as men. No longer do the pensioners file daily into Chapel; but neither do they dine with the Warden on Sundays. Each house is well heated; but no longer can old men warm themselves beside an open fire.

Clun is a little town full of character, of tiny shops and of people chatting at street corners, especially on market-day; people with fresh-coloured, highly individual faces who wore what pleased them and was most convenient, with only a slight regard for current fashion. I loved listening to the soft upward lilt of their voices.

The church, an immensely solid fortress-like affair, standing high above the town, responds well to the challenge of the Castle and of the high, bold hills all round. One gentler rounded little hill just above the town was called Jenny's Knowle.

The Brook runs to the south and before it sweeps round the Castle passes under an ancient bridge, built in the same solid way.

After Clun the Brook widens between the high uplands of Clun Forest. One day I motored a few miles beyond Clun along the road that runs westwards above the river, and stopped at a farm called Lower Spoad beside a great dyke that I knew from my map to be Offa's Dyke. Here I asked permission to leave my car.

'Come and sit you down by the fire a minute and have a cup of tea', said the farmer's wife. She gave me much more than the tea, the warmth of the fire and her friendliness—namely, the chance to see an exciting carving, in oak black with age and smoke. It depicted a boar hunt complete with men and dogs. The boar had just been pierced clean through by a long spear. A wonderful thing to meet so unexpectedly. My hostess also showed me a bit of massive wall among a tangle of bushes in her garden, remains, so folk said, of an old castle that once fortified the Dyke. Lower Spoad now offers rewarding hospitality for the night.

After a grateful goodbye to the farmer's wife I cut down the fields to rejoin the Brook. Beside it stood an arresting, half-timbered cottage; very old indeed, its gabled roof golden with lichen. No human being appeared, but a fierce gander ran after me, hissing and shooting out his neck. I had to walk backwards with my stick thrust out in case he nipped my legs. Caution was needed at all those riverside farms, for nearly all owned a few geese.

Some three or four miles further up the valley, beyond the little village of Newcastle, in a field full of sheep and geese and of ducks sporting in the water, stood a plain solid greystone farmhouse called Hall of the Forest, built in days when there would indeed have been a real forest. I went to it with lively interest one day because of a recently read book called *The Lady of Bleeding Heart Yard*. The lady, Frances Villiers, when only fifteen was forced by her grim stepfather, Sir Edward Coke—a so-called 'vindicator of national liberty'—to marry Sir John Villiers, brother of the Duke of Buckingham. To gain his purpose, Sir Edward tied her to the bedpost and beat her daily till she gave in. From then onwards one storm after another swept over her. Her husband went mad; the Villiers family disputed the fatherhood of her baby; she was excommunicated and imprisoned; condemned to walk barefoot in a white sheet from St. Paul's to the Savoy (a penance which she spiritedly refused to perform); was hunted from one hiding place to another by her implacable relations, till finally, after a hair-breadth escape, disguised as a page, she was carried away in a coach by her lover, Sir Robert Howard, to this remote house on his Border property. Here she probably stayed five years, much of that time alone except for her servants. A romantic story with a romantic setting.

No one was at home. I wandered about and pictured how Frances too, perhaps, did the same; listened to the curlews like myself, and forgot for a while her cruel past. What, I wondered, did the country people think of her? If they were as kindly a race as now, they must surely have been sorry for this lonely girl and tried to befriend her, even if some shook reproving heads over her story.

As familiarity with the Brook increased, and also our love for it, an urgent need to find its source possessed us. So, one April day, the boys and I packed our knapsacks, and Harry drove us as far as Clun, where we took to our feet. Along the western road we trudged, with an occasional backward glance at the Castle, towering dark and impressive above the river. After a couple of miles we struck up the steep hillside to the south and felt our adventure had really started. The day was cold and a north wind blew, but we climbed in the highest spirits, and when we reached the top the boys' exhilaration was immense.

The wild empty hills, the knowledge that we now walked along a high watershed, with the Teme on the left and the Clun to the right, and finally the sight of Offa's Dyke rising in a great dark wave clean across our path—all this was inspiring. The dyke I found, had probably been built by Offa, King of Mercia, in the second half of the eighth century, to mark off and protect his kingdom from the dreaded Welsh. For me, it recalled the dyke beloved in childhood, Wansdyke, which came rolling over our Wiltshire hills. Offa's Dyke, like Wansdyke, will run its purposeful course for hundreds of years yet, and so keep alive the name of a king who did so much to unify England, a king whose reputation, it is claimed, stood almost as high in Europe as that of Charlemagne. Personally, I always picture him now as a towering figure standing on top of his Dyke.

Something else gave me great delight as we climbed another Black Mountain. This was a clump of exquisite yellow pansies, with long upper petals. It seemed incredible that anything so dainty, so delicate, could grow or rather perch in the rough grass on this cold dark hilltop. For they truly looked like butterflies. My flower book later identified them as *Viola lutea*, or Mountain Pansy, and I was to meet them over and over again. The boys were too engaged now in one of their impassioned arguments to throw more than a casual glance at my pansies. Today it was on the rival merits of western and eastern civilisation, and it continued till we reached our destination, the Anchor Inn, on the boundary between Shropshire and Radnorshire.

Because building repairs were in hand it looked a bit desolate at first sight. However, contrary to my usual habit, I had taken no risk about a lodging for the night. An attractive girl seemed really pleased to see us and set out a generous tea with toast, eggs and cake beside the fire. The outside appearance of the Inn mattered no longer.

The boys bolted their food and hurried out into the twilight to find the source of the Brook, but appeared a little upset because nowhere did the water gush freely out in the way they had imagined. It just oozed, a little here, a little there from a bog, in jet black drops. That our lively Brook should start in so tame a way seemed all wrong to them. But when they had followed it a short distance and seen the speed with which it turned into a brisk little stream their spirits returned.

After a huge breakfast next morning we set off on the homeward journey; a complicated and exhausting one because we had decided to take a more southerly line. All went well at first. We followed tiny lanes above the Teme, shining in the morning light and came close above the village of Beguildy, every bit as attractive as its name. But we dare not visit it, for it stood on the wrong side of the river and we should get hopelessly off course. From that time on the tumbled mass of hills conspired to frustrate and mislead us. Because they never followed a clear line there was no continuous ridge to walk on, no valley to stick to. As we zigzagged uphill and downhill, I cursed myself for never having mastered a compass. The bee-line I tried to steer caused an infinite amount of unnecessary exertion. Once it took us up a particularly unfriendly hill, thickly covered with brambles. I sat down at the top to cool myself and free my legs of thorns. Well, I thought, I'm getting old. The boys will think nothing of this. They appeared a few minutes later, red-faced and extremely cross. 'Your bee-lines are abominable!' they said. Why on earth had I led them up such a horrible hill? When I studied the map I found that ironically it was called Mount Pleasant!

From that time onwards our journey grew increasingly difficult. No path would take us the way we wanted. The sun sullenly buried himself behind a mass of dark clouds; the wind blew cold in our faces. When we reached a place called 'The New Invention' (once an inn) an old man looked at us sorrowfully and told us to go a mile back up the road we'd just come by, and turn right beside 'two houses' at the top of the hill. After this we found ourselves in a vast tract of country with no house, no tree, no road in sight, and twilight gathering. Here we might well have wandered all night but for a solitary shepherd. 'You binna where you ought to be', he told us. 'The Cwm—that's where you should make for'. Though the boys bore up well, I was disgusted to find it a terrible effort to place one foot before the other.

We reached the Cwm, a large house down in the valley, in complete darkness. The inmates, in full evening dress and about to go in to dinner, allowed me to telephone to Tom, and kindly gave me a glass of wine and the boys some milk.

In half-an-hour we were on our way home. An ignominious end, perhaps, to our adventure, but it left us with good things to remember. Offa's Dyke, the yellow pansies, tea at The Anchor, Beguildy in the bright morning sunlight; and, not least, the joy of snuggling down into Tom's car. Also, we had the satisfaction of feeling now that we knew our Brook from start to finish.

V

THE HILL AND THE FOREST

The Hill

Though the village was an endearing place, the Hill drew me continually away from it. High, but not too high, just under 1,000 feet; close enough for a quick walk before breakfast or last thing at night; steep, but not too steep to push up a two-year-old or carry her on one's back in gentle stages. Quiet; uninhabited, except for sheep, curlew, small birds, and foxes; covered with grass, bracken, whinberry and heather, it took a hold of me that never loosened.

When, after three years, we moved from our house by the Brook to one higher up the village I could see the Hill plainly from my bed. Dark with rain; or carrying massed cumulus clouds on its shoulder; alight with the newly-risen sun, or shining faintly in the moonlight, it remained always beautiful.

But I loved it best in the early morning. Once I went up on a cold, still autumn day, when the sun was just breaking through the low clouds. Exactly as the clock struck nine it caught the top of the church tower, and away beyond the western reaches of the Brook the fragment of a rainbow suddenly blossomed like a rose out of the mist, quivered there for two or three minutes, and was taken back into the mist.

On another occasion the radiance of the morning tempted me up soon after sunrise, when the Hill threw a deep shadow over the whole village. The harvest moon, three parts full, glimmered overhead, but the sun was still hidden. As I approached the summit the bracken began to burn ahead of me; each leaf a flame. I stepped from the shadows straight into the brightness. Fleecy golden clouds lay along the top of Corndon and the Long Mynd, till suddenly the hills threw them off and stood up triumphantly. A scarf of mist still wound between the terraces of Wenlock Edge.

On top of the Hill two small woods offered shelter from wind and rain; one shaped like a stranded Noah's Ark, the other a humble straggle of firs, beeches, and twisted thorns. When I was driven into it for the first time by a sudden storm, a flock of long-tailed tits flitted musically just above my head, so that I could have touched them if I raised my arm. In a far corner crouched a hare, who had also taken shelter there. The view from the top, so compelling that first evening when we discovered the village, stayed so at all times of day, at all seasons.

Soon I could name each of the multitude of hills that rose and fell on every side. There was the dark peak to the south-west already familiar as the Titterhill, and far beyond it Radnor Forest. West of the village stood Black Hill, solid, treeless, heather-covered, and on the other side of the valley the Stepple, Radnor Hill and Bury Ditches (an iron-age camp). Further west the river valley lost itself in Clun Forest, and beyond that rose Kerry Hill. On the north stretched the Long Mynd, and in front of it reared sharply a wooded hill called the Burrow, topped by another ancient camp. Far to the east soared the Clee Hills. A solid pyramid pushing up in the north-west was the Wrekin. These hills, so individual in shape, changed eternally. Within a single hour they could vanish, solidify under a wild light, dissolve again in mist.

On the south side of the Hill lay Rock Forest, and a path dropped steeply beside the tiny stream that burrowed its way out of the hillside and ran down to join the Brook after its wide bend southward.

If you followed this stream down the hill you came to a straggling wood where a brown owl could often be seen sitting high in a holly-tree. Something else often drew Jill and myself there; two monotonous, resounding 'boomps', like the breathing of two very large hearts. I traced one of them to a mechanical contrivance in the bed of the stream, and the other to a strange straw-bound erection a little distance away. When I first took Jill there she approached this straw-covered, bewhiskered figure cautiously on tip-toe with a tight grip of my hand. She could not persuade herself that it was only a harmless pump for a long time. The strange 'boomp' noise convinced her that it was alive and could hear her coming. But it had a tremendous fascination for her all the same and she often said, 'Mummy, let's go to the Pumps'.

That southern spring was only one of a whole network. When I first met William Gittoes, an old shepherd who lived beside the

Clun at Shepherd's Bridge, fetching a pail of drinking water from the nearest spring, he told me he 'reckoned not many hills had as many springs as this owd hill'.

I have known many shepherds in my life but none quite so fine a looking one as he. Years later I can still see his face as clearly as when he stood beside the spring; the sky-blue eyes, the wide forehead, the silver hair and side-whiskers, the strong, straight back.

The Hill was a grand place if you wanted to meet the wind face to face. One day I woke to hear it stirring and sighing, then rising to angry growls which grew louder and more vicious moment by moment. Finally it reached gale force and surged like a stormy sea, swishing against the house, receding, then returning with a sudden roar. Still munching a bit of toast I hurried up the hill. You could feel, and almost see, its moisture-laden presence streaming down the valley from the western hills. Trees, fields, and hedges lost their separate identity in that wild, on-rushing greyness. Again a rainbow appeared but with nothing poised or flower-like about it this time. It glimmered for an instant, a pale shaft of colour high in the clouds, and vanished. Smoke from cottage chimneys was torn to fragments and scattered across the sky. Crowds of dead leaves pattered down the hill path. From the south side wind-blown children in sou'westers and mackintoshes struggled to the top on their way to school. Only the stolid sheep, threading through the bracken, seemed unaffected. It was an exhilarating walk. But when I reached home a great piece of rough-cast had been torn from the house, and I was met in the doorway by an unhappy, haggard lady who was being treated for nervous trouble. She looked as if her hair was about to be torn from her head. 'Oh!' she gasped, 'This horrible, horrible wind! I feel completely disintegrated!'

In a gentler wind the Hill was a famous place for flying kites, or for a 'kite-walk'. This meant letting your kite rise as high as string would allow and then tramping along the top, keeping it aloft no matter what obstacles you encountered. The victor was the one who succeeded in taking the longest uninterrupted journey. More than one dilapidated kite hung in the trees of Rock Forest for many a year.

In a good season the Hill supplied a moderate crop of whin-berries, and a larger one of mushrooms. I particularly remember a wet spell in October, following a long drought, when Jill and I went up the Hill with baskets. A monstrous cloud enveloped

Black Hill. Soon it rolled towards us and a torrent of rain drove us into the little wood. When it abated we hurried out and found hosts of mushrooms. Jill, in ecstasy, trotted about filling her basket. But some of the bright-coloured toadstools delighted her more; little scarlet and orange ones, bunches of Sulphur-Tufts and best of all a tiny delicate thing the colour of a thrush's egg. Presently we reached a crop of horse mushrooms, and as we squeezed a few into our already laden baskets a woman approached and asked, 'Can you say for sure those are safe to eat?' I gave her a firm assurance.

'That's a mercy!' she cried, 'I want to take a basketful back for my vegetable stall in Liverpool—I've a brother down at Twitchen— and folk are afraid of them and say they're poison. Now I can say they don't know what they're talking about'.

One day as I picked a few young bracken shoots for a salad, the old farmer came riding by on his pony and smiled all over his face. 'You're welcome to as many of those as you like', said he. I think he hoped I would make a real inroad on his farm.

Some people went up to cut a bit for litter for their poultry and pigs, and rolled it in great bundles down the slope.

There were no houses on the top of the Hill, but a few small rock-like dwellings tucked themselves close under it.

Two elderly sisters, Miss Bertha and Miss Winnie Whittall, had spent the greater part of their lives in one such house. Tales of the past poured from them, when, not long after our arrival, I had tea beside their fire. Each kept picking up the narrative from the other, or even snatched it from her lips.

'You're the doctor's wife', said Miss Bertha, the elder. 'Now Mother (she was ninety when she died last year) remembered the first doctor ever to settle in Clunbury. Dr. Mechan was his name. His young wife was a great one for the fashions and wore the first crinoline ever seen in the village'.

'And mother and the other girls', broke in Miss Winnie, 'not to be outdone, cut long stems of briar, rubbed off the thorns, and sewed 'em into the hems of their dresses'.

Miss Bertha took hold again. 'Then Mrs. Mechan startled everyone with white frilly trousers showing beneath her skirts, and she was the first to have a perambulator for her baby. 'Twas made of wicker-work and had three wheels. In those days everyone hereabouts carried their babies in their arms and mothers didn't like 'em to grow too stout because of the weight. Mother told us how she and her friends would watch Mrs. Mechan pushing the pram up the hill with her white trousers shining out against the green grass'.

'We were minded of mother's tale when we saw you taking your little girl up there in her push chair', said Miss Winnie. Then they told me of an old man who remembered the first proper pony-trap ever to be driven up the Clun Valley. Before that everyone walked— 'and my, how they did walk once on a time'—or rode, or drove in old farm carts, because the roads were too bad for anything else. When they began to make them up a bit the carters who brought the stones from the Clee Hills would start off at midnight so as to escape the double toll at the Turnpike.

Soon we were back to the Hill. 'In mother's young days', said Miss Winnie, 'a man called Jimmy the Fiddler lived where Wadsworth's orchard is now. He went to all the villages around playing at weddings and dances and such-like, and folk would see him coming back down the hill with a lantern. When he'd been dead a longish while, mother was on her way home in the twilight with a bundle of sticks, when she thought she saw him slipping down in front of her, with his fiddle under his arm. She was so flummoxed she dropped all her sticks and stood stock-still. He disappeared round the bend at the bottom and she never saw him again'.

No one in the village was so much a part of the Hill as these two sisters.

Rock Forest

As I had anticipated on my first visit, I went to Rock Forest again and again.

One Spring day, a few weeks later, Jill and I carried our tea there. We picnicked on the high slopes in warm sunshine, above hosts of primroses. Deep blue shadows covered the lower part of the Forest and a shimmer of gold hung over the top of the larches. When the sunlight got tangled in their branches it was broken into a hundred flashing stars. Ring-doves cooed continuously.

Jill busied herself enlarging a rabbit-hole with her hands, working busily and patiently for a long time. I think she hoped to go down it in the end. The only thing that interrupted her now and then was the bubbling of a curlew overhead. Each time she heard it she stopped digging and laughed aloud. At last I had to drag her unwillingly home. At the entrance to the Forest we came on a gamekeeper's larder—about half a dozen little owls, as many stoats, two or three weasels, a rat, and, blackest crime, two hedgehogs. As they dangled there in the evening sunlight, with spring newly come to the earth, I felt an intense pang of pity, even for the stoats. Their primrose waistcoats looked so smooth and dapper, as though they had only just groomed themselves. As for Jill, tears were rolling down her cheeks. She was very tired by this time, so I carried her pig-a-back down the hill and told her a story to make her forget the hateful larder.

That was the first of many spring and summer picnics. But the Forest fascinated me at all times of the year.

Once I dropped into the heart of it late in November when all the trees were bare. But in the centre a water-guelder, still laden with shining scarlet berries, glowed against the shadows, and under the sycamores the fallen leaves made a tessalated pavement of white and golden brown. In snow time the little stream ran inky-black under bracken leaves festooned with tiny icicles. Countless birds and tiny creatures left their tracks in the snow, and sometimes a blood-stained footprint trailed sadly away into the undergrowth. Once I came on a hawfinch eating berries under a bush. All the old nests were full of snow.

One January day I set off with an eiderdown as a wedding present for a girl who had worked for me and now lived in a cottage at the bottom of the Forest. When I had lugged my parcel up the Hill I propelled it down the slope with a series of kicks, evoking cries of startled alarm from the birds as the ungainly bundle came lolloping among them. I found the bride picking snowdrops under the trees, while her mother collected sticks. The old lady told me she had lived in that same house when she was a child seventy years ago. Her own mother said that once two cottages stood where the snowdrops now grew, and that in one of them lived an old man who came to a sad end. He bled to death from a wound he made in his leg with his axe while he was woodcutting alone in the Forest. They carried him home through snow so deep that the hedges were almost buried, but he died before they could lay him on his bed. For days a bloody trail lay on top of the frozen snow, her mother told her.

VI

ROUND AND ABOUT

The Rock of Woolbury

After the conversation with the Merediths, I resolved to take the first opportunity to visit the quarry they had spoken of.

There had been a cold spell. Patches of snow lay everywhere on the high lands. But on this particular morning the feeling and smell and sounds of Spring prevailed. The sun shone, birds sang triumphantly, and the familiar cry of the curlew came across the orchard for the first time that year; no bubbling but just the clear musical call. I ran out and caught a glimpse of his fawn wings beating low over the frozen grass. We, that is Jill and myself, would go to the Rock of Woolbury that very afternoon.

But when we tried to motor up the little lane that led towards the quarry, we soon found it completely blocked by snow, and had to reverse down the hill. Undaunted, we started on foot, but before long Jill's gumboot got firmly wedged in a drift. I hurried off to borrow a spade from a farm but when I returned she had cleverly dug it out with her hands. We now plodded along through snow that was often level with the hedges as we climbed higher.

Following Harry's directions we turned off on a path through the woods, and suddenly found ourselves looking down at the quarry. Very grand and impressive it appeared in the dim light, its rocky sides rearing out of deep drifts. We were not foolhardy enough to drop among them, but just stood staring, and I thought what a labour it must have been to cut out all those tons of stone and take them down to Clun, probably on rough wooden horse-drawn sledges.

The rock at the western end had a distinctly sphinx-like look, though the face was of an old man with a knobbly nose. I felt the stone-cutters must have deliberately spared him as the genius of the place. For Jill he was the King of the Quarry. Visible all about us were the footprints of birds and animals but not a living creature. They had wisely taken shelter for the night, which I felt we had better do too, for that lowering yellow sky threatened more snow.

I dragged Jill unwillingly away, promising to return in the summer, which we did, on a delicious, still, hot day. The quarry was full of flowers and of butterflies. At the top of the highest cliff, hidden in the ivy, a kestrel had a nest with young. From the further, we could hear their harsh young voices, and watch the parents flying to and fro.

The Llan

Eight hundred feet up, on the western edge of the parish, stood a farm called the Llan. You approached it by a steep narrow lane and then across fields, full of sheep, that dropped gently to a valley. The yard at the Llan was always alive, and perhaps still is, with geese and ducks and hens. Two sheep-dogs usually lay fast asleep. One of these, though a male, answered to the name of Juno, because the two boys at the farm continually talked to him when they were small, telling him everything, and asking him 'D'ye know this? D'ye know that?'

A flight of steps led up to the old grey-stone house, built with a solidity to withstand all the gales and storms that swept the hills. Another flight of steps led up to one of two barns which framed the Titterhill. The farmer's wife was one of the most dynamic people I have met. Her taut, plump body seemed propelled by an energy that exceeded that of three or four ordinary people put together. When I was sketching in the yard she constantly appeared in the doorway calling in her high voice to the hens and ducks, to Juno, to her husband, or the farm boy. Nothing seemed to daunt her; nothing to shatter her good humour. She worked tirelessly through the day, and later tripped down through the steep wood— usually in high-heeled shoes—to a W.I. meeting, a whist-drive, a dance.

Her husband had a lean, brown face and a most benign expression, and preached at the little chapel at the Twitchen. He was deeply attached to his farm, and said he wouldn't accept a farm in the village, even if it was rent-free.

When I took the first of many good teas at the Llan, his wife's dramatic way of telling a story marked her down for a play as soon as I could get one going.

One of her tales concerned a man named Phillip who courted a maid at the Llan, a great strapping lass. His attentions included the gift of several pairs of silk stockings. She accepted them but they failed to soften her heart. At last, grown desperate, he took her for a walk beside the Brook and told her, 'If you wunna marry me I'll drown myself here before your very eyes'. Once more she refused him and he scrambled down into the water.

'Lor, Phil!' cried the girl. 'You'll have to find a deeper place nor that one!' Phillip came dejectedly out, and shortly afterwards demanded that she either returned the silk stockings he had given her, or paid him back the money he had spent on them. She replied that they were all worn to shreds and that she neither could nor would refund the money.

After tea my hostess took me to look at a strange, rough old stone—a tombstone apparently, under some ancient trees. A large W., a heart, and a star, were carved on it.

As far as I could learn there existed no grounds for believing that once a church had stood there. There are Llans all over Shropshire and Wales. Perhaps someone died there long ago when snow was too deep on the ground to take the coffin to the village, and so he was buried under the trees. I once stayed at the Llan for a night or two, and decided that to occupy the privy gave real pleasure. You reached it along a grass path through a tangle of flowers and vegetables, and then you sat looking out at the Titterhill, and, as likely as not, listened to a curlew.

Llanbrook

In the valley below the Llan lay a little farm called Llanbrook. One Sunday, when Tom was away and a young locum in charge, but out for the morning, a girl arrived with a bulky bandage round her leg. She lived, she said, at this farm, and 'the owd grey cock', a very spiteful bird, had pecked her and drawn a lot of blood. She reckoned she'd need a stitch or two. I comforted her with a cup of tea and some magazines and asked if she was the daughter of the farmer at Llanbrook.

'S'posed to be', was her cryptic reply. But I knew enough now of Shropshire modes of speech not to suspect illegitimacy. Shortly afterwards, while Jill was riding at the Llan, I thought I would pay a visit to Llanbrook and enquire after the cock-bitten girl. So I wandered down the hillside, and crossed a brook into a lane, where immediately four lambs bounded to meet me. They thrust black noses into my hands and even tried to eat the hat I carried, but after accompanying me for some way, they turned aside for a game in the grass.

When I reached the farm I found a woman whom I guessed to be the mother of the girl. Yes, the leg had healed up well. Yes, those were her lambs. Their mothers were two young hogs (year-old ewes) who because of a cruel east wind, caught a cold in the 'elder' so that their milk dried up. Oh yes, no doubt they'd write the word 'udder' in books, but hereabouts the word was 'elder'. She'd fed those four from a bottle, and now they were that tame that often she had to take a broom and sweep them from the kitchen. 'More'n once they'd well nigh burned themselves at the fire, they would press that close looking for the milk I always warm there. A neighbour had two lambs frizzled up like that'.

Oh yes, there was nothing she didn't know about rearing of animals and docterin' 'em and her neighbours as well. She made a drink of wormwood sometimes, when a body needed a tonic, or a nice tea from the mugwort in the hedges. While she talked, with strange intensity, I noticed that her pale blue eyes never seemed really to see me. But all the same she declared herself glad to have a chat, because she had listened to that play we had broadcast about witchcraft. It made her laugh and laugh, and it reminded her of all sorts of things she'd heard as a child about foxglove and elder and such-like. Beyond a doubt there was trees that never ought to be took into the house. Honeysuckle now—she looked at a piece I carried—that was good, but there was others that brought nowt but harm.

And there were some trees must never be cut when the sap was running up-hill. One year her boss began cutting the sallies down by the brook, just in front of the house, at the wrong time, and she'd kept 'craving and craving' at him, but he went on cutting. Then she was took ter'ble bad, and every time he cut a fresh one the pain went through her like a knife. And not till he give over did she get better. It was very near the end of her, by gosh it was!

70

And only last year did she see her neighbour, Jack, drive by with a cart-load of sallies cut when they shouldn't have been and she cried to him, 'Jack, for the Lord's sake stop a-cuttin' them sallies!' But he paid no heed. They were wanted, he said, to mend the fences. To make matters worse what must he do but burn the chips in the house! And sure enough his poor mother was taken mortal bad, and stayed so all the year. And such a lambing they had! Terrible! Which went to show what mischief stubborn folk bring on 'emselves when they wanna harken to them as knows better'.

She spoke with such conviction that for the moment she almost made me believe that she must be right.

Little Flanders

One of my explorings during that first summer led me up a steep narrow lane a few miles west. I never saw a soul till I came to a cottage where, sitting in her garden in the sunlight, was a real old picture-book woman in large white sunbonnet, blue cotton dress, and white apron. She looked as still, as utterly rooted there as if she had herself grown among the tangle of flowers—the stocks, pinks, marigolds and love-in-the-mist. She smiled when I said good evening, but did not speak. I left the lane to wander up a grassy track, beside a stream, past a deserted cottage, where two fluffy baby owls sat blinking on a bush. They were so small that they must have been Little Owls. Still I saw no human creatures except some haymakers far away on the skyline.

A climb up a hummocky field brought me now to the ruins of an old greystone house set among hazels and crab-apples. In what had once been the garden grew gooseberry bushes laden with little golden berries; sweet and delicious. Below the house a stream ran through a dingle, where teazels spread in a miniature forest. As I sat on the grass, eating gooseberries in the evening sunshine, it seemed an enchanting place. Nor was I the only one to think so. A flock of goldfinches busied themselves, twittering sweetly, among the thistles below me; a green woodpecker flew across with a startled laugh. There were greenfinches in the apple trees. Deserted houses, ruined houses, are always fascinating, and this one particularly so. What kind of people had lived in this lonely spot?

When I got home Harry told me I had been to a place called Little Flanders. Once, so it was said, a colony of Flemish weavers set up there and took their cloth to Ludlow market, and bought their wool. How strange, how interesting, if this had indeed been so. The big field would have hummed with activity, the stream in the dingle have been in constant use, and the teazel-heads have served to comb the cloth.

I tried in vain to find out more. All I could learn was that for as long as anyone could remember the place had been known as Little Flanders, and that the weavers were said to have settled there in the reign of Edward III. And the house? Someone had surely occupied it in not-too-distant times? Granny Hughes gave me the answer. A big family lived there many years ago. One day, while the mother was shopping in the village, the children played with a box of matches, and burned down the house.

After that I often went to Flanders to pick the little golden gooseberries, to listen to the laughter of the woodpecker, to picture the Flemish colony living in this lonely place so far from their native land. Life must have been hard for them in any case, and surely made harder still by hostility from local weavers.

Flander's Folly

High on Wenlock Edge stands a half-ruined tower called Flander's Folly. Though I link it here with Little Flanders there is no connection between the two. It first really impressed itself on us as we drove home one frosty January night, and saw the full moon rise exactly behind it, rose-red and faintly blurred by mist, like a huge balloon slowly inflating itself. The tower, hyacinth blue on top of the shining hillside, belonged to a fairy tale.

But its origin, according to Harry, was extremely mundane. A rich ship-owner named Flanders built it for one, or both, of two reasons:

(1) He hoped, when he moved to Shropshire, to watch his ships sail up the Mersey from the top of his tower. Certainly a vain hope.

(2) He wished to make sure that the workers on his estate up there on Wenlock Edge never idled away their time, so he would climb the Tower to keep a check on them. When he found to his vexation that a corner remained invisible he died from vexation.

But I still remembered the Tower as it looked that winter night, and we took a picnic there when summer came. The boys, unhampered by Mr. Flanders' ulterior motives, found it romantic and exciting. They raced up and down the stone staircase flying paper darts at each other from the top, and later, as we lay in the grass, Robin made a story about the Tower for Jill. I fancy that not for long would other children enjoy it as mine did that summer day, for both tower and staircase were in a bad state of repair even then.

Two Border Castles

There were three Border Castles that roused more real affection in me than the famous one that towers above the Teme at Ludlow, or even than the castellated manor at Stokesay. This was partly due to a greater familiarity with them, partly that they were less well guarded, less fenced in.

There was Clun of which I have spoken already.

Hopton Castle—the little castle I noticed among the fields when I first climbed the Titterhill—was the second. I returned to it in early Spring when the old shepherd who went with me to the Obley sale asked me and Jill to tea. After a wintry spell, flowers were bursting out miraculously. Primroses, celandines, white violets, daisies, ground ivy, seemed to be welcoming us from the banks of the narrow lane as we drove along. Another welcome awaited us at the shepherd's cottage, where the daughter made a great fuss of Jill.

As we ate our tea beside the fire, the old man, who had the most perfect manners in the world, but with no trace of servility, talked of country things and particularly of the Castle.

'Best be off to see it now before it grows dark', he said. 'When I was a lad the old folk would tell of how the ghosts of the poor soldiers murdered there, often wandered round at nightfall. Not that I believe it myself. Still, best go in daylight'.

I knew enough local history to understand what he referred to. During the Civil War the Castle, which belonged to a fervent Republican named Wallop, held out with a garrison of only thirty-three men for nearly three weeks under Colonel More of Linley against a far stronger Royalist force, led by Sir Lewis Kirke of Ludlow. When finally hunger forced their surrender, every man was put to death except their leader, because they had continued their resistance in a hopeless position. 'The custom we hold in warres is to punish, and that with death, those who wilfully opinionate themselves to defend a place which, by the rules of warre, cannot be kept'. Thus ran an old edict. Justice seemed to demand that Colonel More should suffer rather than a lot of innocent men, who could 'opinionate' nothing themselves. The little Castle was obviously terribly vulnerable, standing as it does under the hill, surrounded by only a shallow ditch.

Twilight was already falling as we approached. The Titterhill towered dark above it, and shadows had gathered thickly inside, though light still glimmered through the ruined windows. The thought of those unhappy soldiers shut in there, hopeless and starving day after day, haunted me, if not their actual ghosts. As we groped our way among stones and undergrowth, Jill gripping my hand tightly, a calf rushed out and nearly knocked her backwards.

A kestrel cried sharp and shrill from the ivy at the top of the tower. Maybe they have bred there ever since the Castle was largely destroyed after the siege.

I was glad at its unfenced state. So often a well-kept fence serves to shut out more than calves and sheep.

Wigmore was the second Castle. When driving southwards to Leominster and Gloucester I always glanced up at a ruined tower on top of the ridge between Adforten and Wigmore and said 'I must go to it'. But, because of the wealth of alluring places, months slipped by and still I had not been. The floods, followed by keen frost, sent us skating on the frozen water-meadows near Wigmore. As the north wind swept me over the ice in late afternoon I saw the Castle tower black against a fiery sky. A line of trees, blurred by shadows, seemed an army on the march—a Mortimer army, returning, perhaps, from a skirmish with the hated Welsh. The ice-bound field, the dark ridge, the impregnable castle, the burning sky—these so gripped me that on a March day a few weeks later I took the narrow lane from Wigmore village, climbed the hillside, passed under the low arch on the southern side of the castle, and found myself looking up at the ruined, but still immensely solid tower that crowns the highest part of the rampart. On the wall beside it a thick growth of ivy spread itself from one giant stem, and may well have been there for hundreds of years. The Castle is reputed to have been built by Earl William Fitz Osborn 'on waste land called Merestun' in the reign of King Edward the Confessor. It suffered much damage from both Welsh and Danes, and was largely re-built soon after the Norman Conquest. The formidable Mortimers now gained possession of it and from this stronghold they wielded power on the Welsh Marches for more than 300 years. Over and over again the peace of the village nearby was broken by galloping horses and men on the march.

Earl Roger, most powerful, most wicked, of all the Marcher Lords, was not only busy fighting the Welsh, but feasted Queen Isabella, wife of Edward II there. And from here, maybe, he plotted the King's murder. Later his great grandson, Edmund, sullied out to subdue Owen Glendower's army on the banks of the Lugg, near Pilleth, where he was utterly defeated and taken prisoner. His captivity had an amusing sequel when he actually married his enemy's daughter. Everyone will remember the scene of his wooing in *Henry IV*, Part I.

Now, where once was such liveliness, such plotting, such trumpeting, such coming and going, the vegetation spread as it pleased. Wych-elms were in crimson bud, beds of wild arum unfurled under the castle walls, and only the yaffling of a green woodpecker broke the silence. Here indeed was a place in which to give one's imagination free play.

There were no paths, no notices, no foot-prints except those of a flock of sheep driven daily by their shepherd through to a field on the farther side. Deep in the undergrowth a bit of old grating guarded the mouth of what looked a very nasty dungeon.

When next I went to the Castle I took Mrs. Mac. It was summer-time, and the enclosure a mass of wild flowers. I needed a variety for a talk that evening at a W.I., and I found them. Good King Henry grew thick round the gateway, doubtless the Mortimer's cook served it to ward off scurvy. High on the rampart beside the tower flourished a bush of Deadly Nightshade, or Belladonna; no dangerous black berries yet; only dingy purple bells. I think it was not too fanciful to picture Roger Mortimer's Medicine Man using a forerunner of this bush to poison an unwelcome guest, or a dangerous prisoner. Roger was clearly a completely ruthless man.

The tower and the walls were bright with little golden wallflowers. In the enclosure grew big blue geraniums, starry centaury, potentilla, self-heal, wild rocket, agrimony and the claret-blossoms of hound's tongue. Even had I failed to recognise its peculiar mousey spell, it revealed itself all too well by the seeds that clung to our stockings and the hem of our skirts. Mrs. Mac scuttled about picking wild rocket to make a blue dye for her weaving, in the hot sunshine, happy as a child. Shut in by ruined walls and growth of trees and flowers, Wigmore's spell was strong again. Once more the laughter of the green woodpecker rang out, or rather that of many green woodpeckers. The place seemed alive with them. Our flower-picking over, we wandered along the eastern outskirts, and between wych-elms, hazels, and maples, peeped across at Bringewood Chase —the wild place where the children in *Comus* lost themselves.

Back at the farm where we had left our car the woman looked at our flowers and said, 'It's a mercy you weren't bitten by an adder. There's a terrible lot round the Castle this year'. We felt thankful that we hadn't known beforehand.

I must have visited Wigmore at least a dozen times after that and always with fresh gratitude that it remained unfenced and unadopted.

But, when I re-visited it some thirty years later, I realised that wildness and independence can be too dearly bought. So over-grown was the Castle now, that, left to yourself, you would hardly know it existed. An army of waist-high nettles, a riot of elder and bramble, a screen of crippled, close-packed trees combined to thwart your entry. Tower and walls were invisible. Only at a point a little further north could you get a glimpse of them. A vicious growth of weeds smothered the wild flowers, and I listened in vain for a woodpecker.

Because I had found it when wandering off to the south-west of the Castle, up and down through steep woods and across fields, I must say a word about another lost place. This was a small fourteenth-century farm set deep among the hills, and formerly, according to tradition, said the farmer's wife, used as a refuge by a band of Lollards when persecution was at its fiercest. In the kitchen stood a beautiful long refectory table.

It was a fascinating spot, close to the oak-covered hills of Deerfold. Here innumerable deer used to roam, and here so it was said, the last English wolf was killed. When, on this later visit to Wigmore I started to find the little farm again the people in Lingen told me, 'It's no good to go there now, it's been turned into racing stables, and the table sold to America'. Bitter news indeed.

VII

AN OLD MAN 'VERY KNOWING ABOUT COUNTRY MATTERS'

One day the Bobby at Clun gave me the address of an old man 'very knowing about country matters' whom he thought I would like to meet. So as soon as I could I set off to find him with a slip of paper in my pocket inscribed, 'Mr. Powell, Graig Wood, Treverward, Selly Hall'. A look at the map showed me where to leave the main road south out of Clun, and I instantly became involved in a tangle of little lanes, and also a series of enquiries—at stray cottages, at a farm, and finally of a roadmender, a charming debonair person with tanned face and coal black hair, who was whistling inconsequently as though trying out his notes. He'd not lived long in these parts, he said, and had only the vaguest notion of the whereabouts of Graig Wood, but he told me of an old lady who would surely help. Before I left him he pointed to the bluebells in the copse close by. 'Aren't they lovely? Aren't they a picture?' he cried.

I found his old lady at a small farm not far away, a dear, godly-looking creature in a plain black dress and a black and white apron, with fat little pimples on her cheeks and a kind face—not the rather hard one that sometimes goes with people who keep themselves, and their home, as immaculately neat as she.

'Mr. Pow-ell' (that is how it comes from their tongues round here). Oh yes—she'd known him all her life, but now he couldn't get about and she'd not seen him for many a day.

She gave me some vague directions, but at least I laid hold of the fascinating name Skyborry, so when I reached a signpost and read it there I left my car and took the lane that way. Even if it had been the wrong one I think I'd have felt impelled to follow it. This lane was steep, narrow, grass-grown and ran between banks alive with campions, bluebells, stitchwort, wood sorrel, archangel, and moscatel. Lots of ferns, too, still in their tawny bishops' crozier

77

stage. Round me was a constant flutter of small wings, and I caught the flash of a goldfinch or a yellow-hammer, or the warmth of a bullfinch's breast. I thought again, as I often have lately, that never was a spring quite so green, so rich, as this particular one.

I was passing through a country of little knobbly hills that swelled up between higher ones, and were covered with maybushes in full flower, their sweetness intensified by the hot sunshine. Small streams ran down from the higher hills and wandered at will across the road as they hurried to join the Teme. Here and there a grey-stone cottage or small farm looked as if it had grown up of its own accord. Everywhere, flowers, flowing water, movement of birds.

Suddenly round a bend I saw ahead on the hillside a group of small birches that somehow gave me an urgent impression that they had just stopped dancing. Whether it was because they stood in a circle, or because of the golden light, or because of the delicate curve of their slender trunks, or because I was in that mood when everything seems to share one's own happiness I don't know—but there it was. I had never had such a fancy before, and probably never shall again.

Presently as I hesitated at a second cross-roads two young carters came up in a waggon drawn by three horses. They told me to follow them and they would bring me to Graig Wood. I hurried behind them away from Skyborry and thought a little sadly that after all I should never get to it—not this time at all events. As they turned into a farmyard they shouted, 'Go through the next gate'.

This led me down a steep lane dropping to the Teme—I caught glimpses of it shining through thick woods—and so to a cottage with a garden running precipitously to the river. Masses of golden wall-flowers bordered the path.

The door stood wide open, revealing on the dresser a row of little china pots. I knocked and a man's voice said, 'Come in'.

There in the evening sunlight sat an old couple. I knew at once the man was the one I sought. He wore a black cloth Sunday coat, had clear-cut features and an expression of combined goodness and intelligence. He rose as I entered and shook hands as though I was an old friend. Then he introduced me to his sister, who sat with a cup of tea in her hand, and wore dark glasses. 'She is blind', he said in a low voice.

They gave me tea and made me completely welcome, though they must have wondered who on earth I was and what brought me. I explained, and at first the old man seemed puzzled. But suddenly his face brightened and he declared that it must be to listen to the 'Lee-gend' of David ap-Even. 'Please tell it to me', I said. An expression of satisfaction stole over both their faces. They settled comfortably in their chairs and told me the following story— sometimes one taking up the thread and sometimes the other.

David was born up at Skyborry a hundred, no it must be several hundred year ago—but you can see the house still. David worked at a farm close by, and when Llanfair wake came he wanted terrible bad to go it, but the farmer said 'no, he mun stay and scare the crows'. As David was a-scaring 'em an unknown Personage stood beside him and said, 'David, why aren't you at the Wake?'

David answered 'Because of the crows'.

So the unknown Personage said, 'Come with me and I'll shut 'em all safe in a barn'. And this he did.

Then David went down to the Wake and there he met the farmer, who flew into a rage and asked why he'd left his job. So David tells him but the farmer wouldna believe him. So back they goes together, and sure enough when they opened the door of the barn out flew the crows'.

After that the unknown Personage (who, you must understand was the Devil himself) used often to come to David in the fields tempting him to one thing and another, till at last David feared the Devil might get too much for him. One day as he was sowing the wheat the Devil came and asked which he'd choose—the tops or the bottoms of the wheat. The Devil, you see, was very ignorant about country things. So David chose the tops and got the better of the Devil. And another time as he planted potatoes the Devil came again and asked the same thing and David chose the bottoms. So he got the better of the Devil again. And another time, knowing himself master now he set the Devil to carry water in a sieve from Llanfair to Skyborry. The Devil tried hard but couldn't. So David had mastered him again, and wanna afeared of him any more. In his Will he said that when he died his heart was to be flung on the dunghill. A raven and a dove would fight for it, and if the raven won it 'ud mean he must go to 'Uncle Joseph' (his other name for the Devil), but if the dove won, he'd go to a better place.

And his corpse must not be taken through the door or the window, nor carried to church by any road or path, and not buried either in the church or the churchyard. Fearful of the consequences if they disobeyed these directions, his relations took some slates off the roof and lifted his corpse through the gap and then carried him along the dykes. They buried him with his head in the church and his feet in the churchyard. They'd got to do what he said, mind you, for fear he'd put a curse on them. And he lay like that till Llanfair church was restored and the grave disturbed. But the skull was missing, and they say that years ago a man's skull and a great key was found in the cellar of Skyborry, but none could open the door in the cellar that leads—so they say—to an underground passage that goes all the way to Craigdun Rocks above Knucklas, t'other side o' the river. 'And there *is* a hole up there', ended the old man. 'You can see it now, and I've put my stick in and there don't seem no bottom to it'.

'When my uncle worked up at Skyborry', he continued, 'he saw the old book with all the story set down. It tells you the very field where David was planting potatoes when the Devil came to him—above Skyborry on the left of the road to Manaughty— *and* the barn where they shut in the rooks. Below Skyborry that was. It's all in the book. What's the truth of it we *don't* know'.

No, I thought. David carried both the truth and the imaginings away with him when he died.

'But he really lived', the old sister put in, 'and there's a bit of his tombstone still down in Llanfair churchyard with an urn on it, and his head, and a dove and a raven'.

I thanked them for their strange story and promised to visit Skyborry before long—*and* Llanfair churchyard. Then I asked about the little pots on the dresser.

Those, said the old woman proudly, contained a salve she made every spring from primroses and mayflowers boiled in lard. It was very comforting for the rheumatics. She could see just enough to manage with her brother's help. Her blindness was because she had been run over by a cart when a child. It didn't affect her at first, but in Queen Victoria's Jubilee year first one eye went and then the other, and in that year her brother had his left foot shot away.

The baker now arrived, and the old man questioned him eagerly about the auction at Knighton. How were prices today? The old woman asked if he'd seen her niece on the road? He said with a grin he'd seen 'something' coming up the hill. Just after he'd gone in came the 'something'—a pretty, buxom girl of about seventeen, a little shy of me but with friendly simple manners.

When I left they both said, 'Be sure to come again'.

Soon after this, the 'Lee-gend' still in mind, I took Harry and his wife for a jaunt up the Teme Valley, and we stopped at Llanvair (the full name is Llanvairwaterdine). The little church, though much restored, is very old in parts, and we read with interest the names of all the farms in the parish—Garbett, Selly Hall, Garth, Graig, and so forth—carved on the ancient pews. And we tried in vain to decipher an inscription on the altar rails. Then we poked about in the churchyard, and in the long grass Harry found two pieces of a broken tombstone.

'Look!' he called. 'See what I've found!'

We duly made out the name, and a bit of carving that might well have been a raven. The date seemed to have been 1514, but was more likely 1614.

At that time the influence of witchcraft and of belief in direct encounters with the Devil would have still been very strong in that secluded valley.

Mrs. Meredith noted with amusement the old-fashioned look of the people on the roads. 'We've not worn hats like that for five years or more', she declared, 'and just look at the length of their skirts!'

To take those two for a drive was an enriching experience. They noted and commented on all they saw; the look of the corn; the number of sheep; the quality of the shops; the condition of the schools.

The next visit to David-ap-Evan country was with Jill in fulfilment of a long-standing promise for a cycling expedition.

On a blazing August day, as we plodded up Rock Hill I wished I had never made it. Why hadn't we taken a picnic by the Brook and bathed? Done anything but climb this horrible hill? However, 'Skyborry' was still a magic word in my head, the old Powells a happy memory. Fortified by bread-and-cheese and an hour's rest, we set off through the tangle of little switch-back lanes, many too steep for cycling, and came at last to Craig Wood.

The old man gave us a warm welcome and called to his sister, 'Mrs. Doctor Gandy is here'.

They gave us tea and I told them of the discovery of David's tombstone, and asked the date of Llanfair Wake. Mr. Powell did some calculations and then said that Feast Day was August 15th, if so be that was a Sunday, and if not then the first Sunday after the 15th, and the day after that was called 'Monday Wake Day'.

'And dear to goodness', cried his sister, 'if you haven't come on the very day, Only', she added sadly, 'nothing happens now'.

When we told them we wanted to find beds for the night in Llanfair they told us of 'a most respectable body', but when we found her unfortunately her house was full. However, we'd do very well, she said, at The Builders' Arms, a plain little inn on the Knighton-Beguildy road. The landlady, a pleasant woman, agreed to take us.

Jill bathed in a pool in the Teme with two small girls staying there, while I wandered by the river.

After a supper of eggs and bacon, Jill made me finish the story of Theseus and the Minotaur (she'd carefully brought Tanglewood Tales in her knapsack). When I said, 'Bedtime', she looked at me suspiciously. 'What are *you* going to do?' she asked.

I said I was going up the big hill we could see from the bedroom window—Beacon Hill.

'Let me come too', she pleaded. I refused. 'Please, please!'

Like a fool I stuck to my refusal. What idiots mothers are sometimes! When I stood on top of the Hill in the twilight and saw a great red moon rising and mist wreaths forming in the hollow, and the Teme shining from the valley, and heard curlews calling sleepily all round, I knew I'd robbed her of something to which she'd as much right as I—and all for a stupid convention that children must always go to bed at the right time!

I hoped to show more sense in future.

Next morning the Beacon wore a skirt of mist and a delicate film lay over the river, but there was every promise of a perfect day. When Jill had bathed again with her friends and had ridden their pony, we set off on our bikes for Skyborry, on the left bank of the river going towards Knighton. We found the place where David's employer had lived, standing a little back and well above the road; an attractive, half-timbered house. But unfortunately the lady of the house was busy cooking. She sent a message by her little maid that if we returned in the afternoon she would show us the house. This would be too late for us, so we consoled ourselves by visiting the barn where the Devil imprisoned the crows. It was certainly ancient enough, of solid oak with fine beams. Jill, who took the story very seriously, planned just how the crows would perch along them.

'I want to read that old book Mr. Powell told you about', she said. I promised to try to find it but somehow never did.

Those were the first of many visits to Graig Wood—to introduce Tom, to take books, to listen to country news. One day I followed hard on the District Nurse who told how, as she was cycling home the previous night in the moonlight, she heard near Treverward Wood as much grunting as would come from a herd of pigs.

'That's a famous place for badgers', said Mr. Powell. 'There's no harm in them—no harm at all. They never take lambs—not healthy ones. I mind another wood with a great big set in it, and below it a pasture beside a brook. And the farmer always put his lambs there 'cos it was such a luscious pasture. And he ne'er lost a lamb—ne'er a one'.

I spoke of my rambles in search of otters, and he told how one night recently a man, going on his motor-bike over the hill between Knucklas and Llangunllo had run against something hard and been lifted clean off his bike, but had landed safely on the saddle. He walked back and found a dead otter, nigh four feet long. Never said the old man had he heard tell of one so far from water.

He went on to remark what a lot of herons—cranes, he called them—he had seen flying over that year. More'n he ever remembered before. 'There did use to be a cranery near Beguildy and the man who took me there sez, 'D' ye know how them birds manage their legs. Why, they make a hole in the middle and stick them through it'.

' "Well", I sez, "and what happens to the eggs?" He couldna say about that'.

The old lady was very quiet that evening because of a recent fall. 'Something come over me and down I went'.

But before I left she asked if I'd yet been up to find the great hole in the rocks above Skyborry. 'The Lee-gend' often came into her mind, especially after repeating it to me.

Of all my visits none is clearer than that first one. Though thirty years have passed since then, I have only to shut my eyes and sit back in my chair to see the old couple in the evening sunlight, the air sweet with wallflowers, while they tell me their tangled tale, first one, then the other. It was for them a treasured personal possession, and their manner of telling it gave it—in spite of its many absurdities —a strange reality.

VIII

OVER THE HILLS

The Titterhill and Black Hill

After I had first looked at it from the top of our Hill, the pointed peak called the Titterhill drew me irresistibly. In less than a month I answered its call. A bitter east wind had blown for days and snow still lay under the hedges and outlined the bases of the hills. I took a bee-line westwards across the meadows, up through steep oak-woods and down a grassy hillside into the next valley.

Small grey farms popped up between the trees and a tempting little ruined castle. But time was short and nothing must prevent me from scaling my hill, standing grand and formidable against a yellow sky straight above me now. Through birch woods, through snow-drifts, and there I was on top of it. No trees grew up here; only heather, glossy red whinberry leaves, and trails of stag-moss showed up where the snow had been swept clean away. Other hills rose on every side, some either capped or delicately patterned by snow, some so far away, so etherialised by the east wind, as to be barely distinguishable from clouds. One day I would identify them all, but the piercing cold discouraged geography, and I nipped home as fast as I could go, plunging recklessly, shoes full of snow, straight down the steepest part. Harry was feeding the pig when I crossed the yard.

'They reckon you can see thirteen counties up there', he said. That was the first of many visits to the Titterhill in all weathers, at all seasons.

It was on an April day that the boys and I went for a picnic and met an Empress on top of the hill; that is to say a female Emperor moth, though we could not then identify her. She had just emerged from her cunning brown cocoon and clung to a sprig of heather, her delicate purple-grey wings drooping moist and limp.

84

We sat down to watch her. For some time she stayed completely passive, and we were growing impatient when suddenly a wave of electric energy swept through her. Her wings vibrated with strange intensity. The sunlight played through them and revealed an exquisite design of four black eyes. It was like the wakening of the Sleeping Beauty, only no Prince was visible. For a moment she seemed about to fly away, but soon relapsed into her former lethargy.

As Oliver laid her gently in a box on her sprig of heather vague discomfort filled me, quite unconnected with his action. Why on earth was this? A newly hatched moth ... a baby about to be born. Instantly the two linked themselves together. I remembered in a flash that just before we left home, in all the flurry attendant on preparing a picnic, I had taken a telephone message. Mrs. So-and-so had started her pains and would the doctor go to her as soon as he returned? And I'd forgotten to write it on the slate!

Panic filled me. Suppose the mother or the baby, or both, died in consequence! I ran faster down the hill than I'd run for a long time, hardly stopping till I reached Hopton Castle, and asked at a farm to use their phone. Lizzie answered me. No, doctor was not back yet; she'd tell him directly he came in. When we got home that evening I questioned him anxiously. There had been no cause for alarm. He had included the expectant mother on his morning round. The baby showed no intention of being born for some hours yet. My relief was intense. I could think about our moth again.

Oliver was already busy with his Moth book. 'Look, look!' he cried. 'Here she is!—a female Emperor Moth!

'And listen to this', he added. 'A freshly-emerged female moth will as a rule attract as many of the opposite sex as one would care to take; all that one has to do is to carry her in a box to some likely spot, and there await the coming of the males'.

After that, though it was growing late, nothing would keep him from going straight up Clunbury Hill with his precious Empress. But he came back in about an hour looking a little sad and cold (an east wind was rising) and reported that not a single male had appeared, though once she had made violent signals with her antennae. To comfort him I promised we'd take her back next day to the Titterhill. This we did. Unfortunately it was colder still and the east wind was in full blast. In spite of it we carried our Empress to the topmost peak and set her carefully down in the heather. There she hung, demure and staid. Surely here, in her own kingdom, those handsome gallant males would come to court her? An hour passed. Nothing happened till, unexpectedly, she began to lay a batch of eggs. Then she stayed motionless again.

We waited another hour, one keeping watch beside her while the other roamed in search of those laggards who, so disappointingly, never appeared; probably because of the east wind and the sunlessness. It can be cold on the Titterhill!

Reluctantly, we left the Empress enthroned in the heather, hoping that perhaps when the sun shone the lovers would arrive. How aggravating, though, never to know.

To face a high wind on the Titterhill was a terrific experience. Once I climbed in a westerly gale which almost knocked me backwards as I reached the top. I could lean against it without falling. The whole world seemed spinning below the racing clouds. Arrows of light struck far-off hills and flew on again. The sun, glimmering whitely as a moon, peered out for a moment from behind a curtain of cloud, then withdrew.

Once, after a whole day spent in Shrewsbury on Women's Institute business, I felt a longing for the Titterhill, motored to Hopton Castle, and climbed the southern side. On the higher slopes I stood in a strange mixed world of light and darkness. In the east the sky was luminous and rosy; light flowed from it as though it was morning. But all the northern and western sky was leaden grey or deep, dark brown.

Over the Teme Valley hung a curtain of cloud, jagged and frayed at its lower edges. Torrents of rain must be falling there. Sometimes the clear half of the sky gained ground; light increased; small birds piped from the black trees. Then the darkness would deepen and the piping cease. The only sounds now would be the roar of the wind and the plaintive bleat of a lamb in the valley. It seemed almost like a stupendous piece of music. As I got higher up the hill, still patched with snow, the blackness and sense of impending storm grew every moment and I turned and ran for my car—reaching it just as rain began to fall in torrents.

Something I shall never forget was a rainbow over the Titterhill. I had been for an October ramble up the peak and down the other side after an unusually wet season; had followed a tiny stream;

had listened to a pair of buzzards and to the sound of running water on every side; had paddled my feet and drunk handfuls; finally had dropped to a smooth green meadow where all the sunshine and peace in the world appeared to be gathered. It seemed like a miniature Garden of Eden, guarded by a single oak in the middle. My stream grew larger and larger till it joined a bigger stream—the Redlake. Beside a waterfall I picnicked and fell asleep to a chorus of robins. A cold drop on my forehead woke me, and a minute later hailstones drove me deep among the alders. The air was icy. Soaked and miserable, I started back up the hill. Where was my Garden of Eden now? Still there but white with hail, and from the whiteness sprang a rainbow. It mounted up the fern-covered hillside and made a burnished pathway before me. To see it always just ahead lightened my climb and warmed my heart.

In autumn and winter the Titterhill could be bracing, exciting, sometimes even magnificent.

But Summer, of course, brought us the happiest days. In a copse on the southern slopes you could hear—and see, if you sat very still—a grass-hopper warbler. There were curlews galore on the western slopes, and usually at least one pair of buzzards. Wild strawberries and whinberries made the hill more desirable than ever.

A monstrous summer partly redeemed itself by the wealth of wild strawberries that sprang up where an oak coppice had recently been cleared away and small larches planted—larches destined to spread in time and with other conifers to ruin our hill. This we did not foresee and all we thought of then was the delight of finding so rich a harvest of berries growing from a carpet of wild sage and herb robert. Many were as large as cherries, and you could kneel down and fill your basket in no time at all. The more it rained the more luscious they became. There came a week when Jill and I picked a bowlful for supper each evening and made ten pounds of jam as well.

I remember particularly how, after a morning of drenching rain, a burst of sunshine in the afternoon sent us hurrying up the hill. For the first time we had company. A few children, purple-faced after whinberry picking, joined us and began gobbling up the strawberries with delighted cries. 'Why', said one, 'the ground's fair *clatted* with them!'

When we had picked at least two pounds, we climbed to the peak for a picnic tea. Never had the view seemed so beautiful. Though the sun shone, clouds still packed the sky, so that all the tumbled hills, rising and falling wave on wave to the horizon, took on an unusual richness and variety of colour. Indigo and peacock gave place to violet and sea-green, and these to palest blue and grey. Ghostly peaks started up from low lying clouds, took substance and vanished, only to pop out again a few minutes later.

The Brecon Beacons thrust up far away to the south-west, the Black Mountains were clear cut; the Malverns dim but definite. Further west rose the pale Cotswold table-land. High mysterious hills swam into view north-west of Corndon—perhaps Mod Sych and Cader Fronwen this side of Lake Bala.

When we looked at a map later we felt we had at last identified those thirteen counties that Harry spoke of—namely Hereford, Monmouth, Brecknock, Radnor, Cardigan, Montgomery, Merioneth, Cheshire, Stafford, Worcester, Warwick, Gloucester *and* Shropshire.

The flowering grass was soft and shimmering in the evening light as the breeze ruffled it. The fierce bees who haunted the peak were there again, and intimidated us whenever we tried to reach the top. The path home down the western side was black and slimy from the footsteps of all the whinberry-pickers who had trodden it in in rainy weather for a fortnight.

During an idyllic summer a bountiful crop of wild raspberries succeeded the strawberries, and again we made many journeys to the Titterhill.

One morning I got up when it was only half light. As I passed the little castle a number of calves peeped out at me from the doorway, followed behind for a short way, then scampered back.

Up on the hillside the dew formed a silver film; the valley below was a sea of mist. I settled down beside a fruitful clump of bushes and began to pick with early morning ardour. A lark let fall a few broken notes; small birds twittered in a subdued way; a flock of sheep lay placid and silent in the field below. We were all waiting for the sun. Suddenly there he was, a flaming ball on top of Stokesay Hill. Immediately the birds sang louder, the sheep got up and lifted their voices in a deep baa of salutation. All the mist in the valley turned to fire—rolling masses of red-gold fire. I stood entranced, raspberries forgotten. But when the glory faded I picked five pounds.

After strawberries and raspberries, the Titterhill offered whinberries, but they were an unpredictable crop; abundant one year, scanty another, and they had to contend with two hazards; pigeons and gipsies. Hilda Gittoes, an indefatigable whinberry picker, told me, 'Those great greedy birds guzzle whenever they have the chance and eat till their crops look nigh to bursting. And as for the gipsies, drat 'em, they sleep at night where the fruit is thickest and are out before we can get on the hill, combing the plants with their horrid little combs and spoiling the plants for next year'.

All the same she picked 150 pounds that particular year, and sold them at fourpence or fivepence a pound to the dealers.

In Birmingham, however, they fetched a shilling a pound. That was the price they earned during the First World War, when the fruit was in great demand for dye. People reckoned then that at least £600 came into the parish from whinberry-picking. Big sums were earned by two sisters who would carry home sixty pounds daily from Black Hill, which bore a bigger and more easily obtainable crop than the Titterhill. To Black Hill, too, went a mother with her eleven children. One of these loved to talk about it. 'Mother would take the whole lot of us, all but the lit'lest, together with a pail of new potatoes boiled the evening before. We'd eat every one and then fill the pail with fruit. Mother, she'd keep us picking till evening came, and my word, it was good to drop into a chair by the fire and eat Welsh cakes when the day was over'.

Once there was a regular shindy on Black Hill. The villagers possessed an ancient right to cut peat there, a right enjoyed by all the adjoining parishes, and actually they used this right to go on Black Hill as soon as the whinberries ripened. But one year the landlord chose to close it when there were grouse about, and the keeper received orders accordingly.

Hilda, her blue eyes flashing, gave me a spirited account of what happened when he tried to interfere with herself and her friends. 'He thought to scarify us, but we took him and "bamboozled" him in the heather. There were six of us and we showed we'd stand no nonsense!'

Once when I climbed the Titterhill to pick a few berries for a tart, I met a mother with six children, all armed with old syrup tins.

'We picked twelve pounds in the first two hours', she told me, 'but the little wretches have wandered off now, and precious few berries will find their way into my basket when my eye isn't on them'. Later I saw the children, more scantily clad now. Some lay blissfully sunning themselves in the heather; some knelt beside the spring squashing berries into their tin mugs and topping them up with water.

'Making wine', they said. Their faces were stained a brilliant purple. It was a very hot day and they, those six and many others, had shed their garments one by one like flowers their petals. From the little fir trees among the heather fluttered gay dresses, skirts, jumpers, vests and stockings.

One hot July, when Jill was six years old, I kept a promise to go right away over the Titterhill with knapsacks and sleep out for the night. All went well till a widish stream blocked our path. Jill made what I thought an unnecessary fuss about crossing it. 'Come on!' I said. 'Throw your knapsack over, take a good run and jump!'

After further appeals, met by a show of obstinacy on her part, she crossed it safely, but flung her knapsack into the water. I'm not sure it wasn't on purpose to mark her displeasure. I fished it out and wrung her dripping pyjamas as dry as I could. It grew warmer and warmer till Jill began to flag a bit. I told stories and hoped we might soon find a resting place for the night.

About five o'clock, we climbed a steep little lane and saw a white house with a particularly pleasant-looking girl in the garden. Seeing us standing by the gate she came to speak to us, and I diffidently asked whether it might be possible for us to stay the night? We'd walked eight miles or so and Jill was tired. When I saw the smile that spread over her face I felt hopeful.

'Wait a moment while I ask my mother!' she said. Back she came to announce, 'Mother says she'd like you to stop with us'.

All went perfectly from that moment. The mother proved the sweetest creature, and treated us almost as though we were expected and welcome guests. A delicious tea in a big cool room, then rest in the garden. Jill, a little drooping thing when we arrived, fairly blossomed out. A seal was set on our new friendship when I mentioned Tom's name. They had heard only good of him.

Jill went early to bed; the walk, though not too long for her, had been hot and steep. Then the daughter, Sally, and I went off with pails to draw water from a spring about a quarter of a mile away. They were dependent on this for all their drinking water. It gushed from the side of a little wood, among a wealth of polypody ferns.

The father, who farmed the surrounding land, came in as we sat down to eggs-and-bacon and country talk. Later he insisted I must taste his currant wine, and his wife, her cherry wine. I had to climb the narrow stairs to bed with the utmost care.

Next day Sally walked with us by a cross-country way round a sharp bend called Fiddler's Elbow to Clun, where we picked up Tom at his surgery and were driven home.

How lucky we had been! A casual pair of strangers couldn't often expect such reception we had. Of course it was all because of Jill. If you want to be sure of getting taken in somewhere have a small, fair, curly-headed girl with you, carrying a knapsack, and looking rather wistful.

One evening during a fine dry spell I was gardening when a strong wind sprang up, and set a pack of dark tattered clouds flying over the hill. Away in the west appeared a still denser pack —so dense that I wondered whether it was cloud or smoke. Could my beloved Titterhill be on fire? I hurried off to investigate. 'Noa, Noa', declared an old farmer whom I met in the lane, "Tis only a storm blowing up'.

But I was not convinced, and when I spoke to the roadman at the Twitchen he told me that the afforested part on the western side of the Titterhill was all ablaze. Much troubled I returned over the top of Clunbury Hill and saw the whole western sky thick with smoke. I heard later that there had been a huge fire, that it had swept over the peak and advanced eastward till it seemed that Hopton Castle—both castle and village—were in danger. Trenches were quickly dug, and everyone prepared for the worst.

Then suddenly in the evening the wind dropped, and the first rain for a month fell. The little Castle was safe, and the villagers could sleep soundly that night. But a host of young trees were damaged and the Titterhill looked very black next morning.

The Titterill is a sadly changed place since those days. The little firs and larches that seemed so few and so harmless, have multiplied into a dense forest. The distinctive shape of the peak is lost. There are no berries to be picked; no place for a picnic.

Clun Forest

I have spoken of the mass of hills that rose and fell temptingly in all directions.

Tom motored up and down the smaller nearer ones to his patients—sometimes thirty miles (there and back) on a single visit. But he seldom joined our longer expeditions. In his free time he hurried to the Brook either for trout or grayling.

Clun Forest was the nearest of the wilder hill-country. It is an upland of some 12,000 acres rising high between the Teme and the Clun and cradles innumerable small streams that hurry down little secret valleys and dingles.

Though much of the Forest is cultivated, and, to an increasing extent, afforested, in our day at all events one could find wide tracks of heather and or of sheep pasture. Our explorings constantly led us to some rewarding spot, some place that seemed far removed from the busy life of the valley.

Once, when I had gone alone for a quiet day in the Forest, had left my car above Newcastle, and wandered westwards up a small cwm, I came on a young man sitting outside a little farm dreamily playing a melodium. He told me he had recently bought it just to make himself a bit of music.

On my way back in a roundabout way, I passed a farm in another cwm, where an old man sat on a bench with a child. He was staring out across the hills and did not notice me till the child nudged him. 'Stay Bank' was the name of the place, he said. Just below him ran a small brook full of mimulus, ducks, and fluffy-haired children paddling. Further down, the mimulus grew in big golden mounds. A glorious mass of it. All round curlews called.

In the lane I surprised a red squirrel with an extra-white tail. The poor little fellow hesitated and looked worried, because I stood between him and the only bushes. So I had pity on him and went back till he made a safe retreat. Further on I stopped to pick wild raspberries, and dislodged a buzzard in the hedge. He looked enormous as he rose so close that I could have touched him. I don't know which of us was the more startled.

One of my most memorable discoveries was the Cantlin Stone, in the company of little Mrs. Mac. We had motored up a grass-grown road beyond Newcastle for about 400 feet to the Riddings, left our car by a farm, had tea in the heather, and then climbed by a pleasant winding track to a point marked 1,600 feet on the map. All along the way grew quantities of that charming mountain pansy first met with near the Anchor. Most of them were daffodil yellow, but some were cream, or blue-and-purple. After a while we reached a pinewood; very dark inside, with hardly any grass under the trees, but many ferns, including Shield Fern and Oak Fern. The wind was humming its special pinewood tune.

We were making our way back by another path when we saw a tall grey stone cross rising from the heather above us. We found it ornamented by a beautiful pattern of twisting snakes and apples, and on a rough stone below it was carved in childish, uneven letters:

'W.C. Decesed here Buried 1691 at Bettws'.

I went home intent on finding more about 'W.C.' and why he had been buried in so lonely a spot. It seemed he was a pedlar named William Cantlin, who roamed the hills carrying a brass-bound box of cutlery and trinkets. One day a stray passer-by discovered his dead body in the heather, and beside him his box. The lock had been burst open and it was empty. Had some covetous wretch given him a knock-out blow and robbed him, I wondered, or had a casual traveller, finding him dead, helped himself to the contents of the box? No one will ever know. There were no detectives in those days, and unexplained deaths must have been all too frequent.

After the finding of the body a dispute took place as to who should bury the poor pedlar. No parish wanted the trouble and expense, except Bettws-y-Cryn, a small village on the other side of the valley. Under the Clun Forest Enclosure Act of 1875 Bettws gained several hundred acres by this good deed because, said the Commissioners, the grave should be brought within its bounds.

Long after Cantlin's death the local M.P., Beriah Botfield, erected the cross on the hillside.

Offa's Dyke, the great dyke first met on our way to the source of the Brook, cuts across the Forest from north to south. Sometimes, when you walked on top of it, you seemed poised between two worlds. Perhaps you would be going northwards, and all the country immediately to the east, peaceful, clear, sunlit. But to the west, where Radnor Forest lay, a ragged indigo curtain might suddenly be drawn across the sky, and blot out everything below. You wondered which side would prevail. Would that threatening cloud unroll still further and swamp you, or would you be able to continue serene and warm, in the sunshine?

Today the only risk you run up there is a soaking. But eleven hundred years ago if you were a Welshman come up from the west a bloody end might await you. From the bottom of the Dyke might spring a small band of English to cut off your head on the spot. Or, a hundred years later, in King Ethelbert's time, they would rid you of your right hand.

No fierce people now, but sometimes interesting ones, odd ones.

On a summer evening I left the Dyke to follow a parallel track and fell in with a swarthy, curly-haired young man named Victor, driving his cows from a field below. We began to talk and I found him a bit of a reader. He had just finished *Jane Eyre* and intended to see the film when it came to Knighton. He thought it a good tale, a strange tale. Often during the winter months he was short of books, so I promised to bring him a few when I next walked that way. He told me where he lived, and called 'Cheerio! not to forget the books!' as we parted.

I tied a knot in my handkerchief immediately. But it was January when I next went to the Dyke. At first I tried the wrong house and was turning away, when the woman who opened the door begged me to come in. Visitors were a treat and I became a doubly worth-while one when I said I carried books. Her husband loved reading, and never wanted to listen to the wireless if he could lay his hand on a book, no matter what. Not long ago he went to a sale, bought a lot of old books for a shilling, and read every word of them. She herself was fascinated by the bird-book I had brought. Never had she seen one before. She turned the pages eagerly till her eyes alighted on a goldfinch.

'Blessed if that's not the bird that feeds in the yard with our hens when I'm throwing out the corn. Now I can put a name to him'.

I found Victor in his bungalow not far away, but so changed from the sunburnt, buoyant fellow I had met beside the Dyke that summer evening I hardly recognised him. He looked pale and heavy-eyed, and had a bad cold. He took me into a cheerless, fireless little room piled up with sacks, where we talked of birds, in whom he also was interested. This started after he had read an article about the habits of the Little Owl.

'They're queer customers', he said. 'There's one sits up on a post who won't take his eyes off me. I have to keep looking back at him whether I want to or not'.

His own heavy eyes brightened as he talked. He had seen no one for three days he said. He told me how, in summer, nightjars came to the hillside below him, and made the rummiest noise he had ever heard. He took my books eagerly, especially the bird-book, which he promised to pass on to his neighbour.

A bitter blast swept along the ridge as I went home. No sunlight now on either side. The Clun and the Teme Valleys alike were darkened by constant storms. The ground grew white with hailstones. You need a stout heart and a strong body to face winter if you live near Offa's Dyke. Not many people lived so close to it as Victor, but small farms or cottages were scattered below it.

One day I drove the Merediths to visit a cousin at a place mysteriously called Newfoundland, a mile or so east of the Dyke. I left them at a cottage by a stream in a little green valley, and went off in search of a badger-set they had told me about. As I climbed the hillside, I saw a little man sitting beside a pond playing with his boots. He had round blue eyes in a sunburnt, simple face, and looked up at me from under a golden-brown felt hat that age had raised to a high peak. His clothes were stained and faded to the same colour mixed with an earthy red. He would have made a wonderful William for *As You Like It*. We exchanged a 'good day', and then edged away from each other in different directions, each, I think, a little apprehensive of the other, each glancing back at intervals to see what the other was up to. He was such a *very* odd little man, and no doubt thought me an odd woman.

I found my badger-set in an impenetrable mass of undergrowth, and then lay down in a bluebell wood. There was such a shimmer on the young birches overhead that white flowers seemed to be growing among them. A fountain of song flowed from a blackcap. Below curlews bubbled. An occasional shadow flying over the bluebells betrayed the passage of some big bird—once a kestrel, then three young crows trying out their wings from a neighbouring tree top.

As I returned to the valley to pick up the Merediths, I fell in with a jolly plump wife from the farm close by. She had never seen the badgers herself, but the other night she had heard one making a fearful noise, 'screaming like a terrified child', she said. The funny little man whom I had met was walking through the wood at the time and now came tearing down the hillside.

'Lor, missus', he said, 'I did believe a wolf was after me!'

I decided I should not be afraid of him any more after that. His brother, also a funny little man, but not *so* funny, wearing spectacles and a slightly less battered hat, went by while we talked, and murmured 'good evening'. Our friend assured us the family was harmless, though simple-minded. There had been three of them, and they lived in a dilapidated house on top of the hill. The third brother had been missing ever since the previous August till a few weeks ago. Then someone, riding through the heart of the wood, came down and said, 'Lor, there's an awful stink up there—must be a dead sheep'.

They found his body deep among the undergrowth.

In the field below an ancient grey horse was grazing—an old war horse, said the farmer's wife, twice wounded. He had been put in the care of a major at Llandrindod, but this man, 'unlawfully, mind you', had sold him to her husband. A colonel from the War Office came down each quarter to make sure he was well cared-for, and when he died they had promised him honourable burial. If ever that old horse heard a bugle blow, or when the children took a gramophone out to the field and put on a record of bugles, he would start to attention, put his feet as close together as he could— just like a soldier, she declared—and stand dead still.

We talked for quite a long time. She used a wealth of country words and expressions, and was obviously happy and completely satisfied with her own way of life, truly a part of her own countryside. She expressed its colour and richness. She rejoiced in it and asked for nothing better. It was not so with all the people I met.

One autumn afternoon I set out with a parcel of books for the Powells, not by my usual route but by a bee-line over the hills. At a house in a clump of Scots pines the only sign of life consisted of a flock of ducks and hens, and two big pinafores floating gently on a line—one deep purple, one peacock blue. I crossed Offa's Dyke and reached a farm named, according to my map, Selly Hall. An ominous curtain of chocolate-brown cloud was drawn across the heavens, but under it the sky shone molten gold, and this brightness caught a great heap of straw, several red and blue waggons, and a lot of gobbling white ducks, all seen against the background of a fine barn. Straight across the yard stretched a row of stone pillars linked at one end to a greystone tower, and carrying on top of them an iron rod. Below the tower, in a small open-ended barn, hung a water-wheel, clearly meant to work the rods, but motionless now. Both house and yard seemed completely deserted. This queer set-up so interested me, however, that later I questioned Mr. Powell about it.

'Ah yes', said he, 'at Selly Hall some years ago lived a farmer who thought he'd make bone-meal for himself and 'twas he put all that up'.

From Selly Hall I climbed through a field of sheep, to another farm right on the Dyke. Here I had to keep a flock of geese at bay with my stick as I crossed the yard to ask for a drink of water. A nice, youngish, dark woman in a grey dress with red buttons—very plain and good—told me this was Garbett Hall and fetched me milk instead of water. When I said, 'What beautiful country you live in!' she answered rather sadly, 'Do you think so really? Would you like to live here yourself?'

I confessed that I wasn't sure.

By this time the sun was very low and I realised I could never reach Graig Wood, before dark. I showed her my parcel of books and told her whom it was for. 'Mr. Powell', she said. 'We all know him round here. My little boy passes close to his cottage on his way to school at Llanvair. He'll be pleased to take it'. As I turned for home she said, 'It's nice to have talked to you. I'd like to get about like you'.

As I climbed the hill a family of magpies floated by and a buzzard made me jump when he shot out of the heather at my feet. He had evidently settled there for the night. The sun, fiery-red in a field of grey cloud, was just setting.

Again the low light lit up the world about me. In the middle of the yellow bracken two tawny-orange sheep stood on a patch of bright green grass beringed by scarlet and yellow fungi. In the half-light the colours were enchanting. Night had fallen by the time I reached the car. Close by sounded the sharp 'te-whit' of one owl and the long wavering 'te-whoo' of another. Once more I had entered for a short time the life of that rich country between Clun and Teme, where some were happy, some frustrated.

Numerous gipsies camped in the small bye-lanes round the Forest when the season for the May Fairs began. Bishops Castle, Ludlow, Craven Arms, Knighton and Clun each had its Fair in succession. People from all the villages for miles around flocked in to ride on the roundabouts, have their fortunes told, see the Fat Lady, buy gingerbread and the clever toys that the gipsies made. Particularly we liked some little brightly-coloured birds of finest plywood with feathered tails that fluttered from the end of long sticks.

One May evening Jill and I lost our way in a tangle of small lanes up behind Clun, and found them alive with gipsies. They were picnicking on the grassy borders or wandering along with their dogs. The children, with heads of wild black hair, kept stealing from holes in the hedges to look at us. Horses and ponies, many of them piebald, strayed all over the place. The women threw at us those compelling, yet at the same time resistible, glances in which they excel, and we drove on till we reached a little farm where, in a yard ankle deep in mud, an old man sat on a log cleaning his boots. When he'd told us the way, I said, 'Cleaning your boots for Sunday?'

'I dunna know so much about cleanin' 'em for Zunday. I be cleanin' 'em 'cos I got such a zore foot', said he.

We brought back many things from the Forest. Whinberries; bunches of cotton grass; sunburnt faces. But more particularly where I was personally concerned, good memories of long days either alone or with the family.

One is of Oliver running nimbly backwards down the steep hillside above Sarn with reckless spinning movements and loud hoots. Once, we were told, a man and his pony had fallen to their death on this very hillside, so I watched his antics with slight apprehension. But his feet, with peculiarly high arches, always kept a remarkable grip.

On a day when Jill had spent much time tumbling in the heather her hair was sweet with the pollen as I kissed her goodnight.

These, and many other things, built up a pattern of wildness, peace and utter content.

Radnor Forest

Radnor Forest provided more wildness and less peace than Clun Forest. It was too rugged, too full of bogs, too rent by deep gullies and chasms, and offered too small a chance of shelter from storms, for that. But we loved it. Personally I never felt such a quickening of spirit, such happy anticipation, as when we hurried off across the Teme, and made for the little market town of Knighton, gateway to the Forest. Sometimes we turned up the steep street, through the Market Place, and so away to the northern boundary. Or—more frequently—we struck south, along a little switch-back road, running between a tumble of hills that grew steeper and steeper as our course became more westerly.

When a high conical hill called the Whimble floated into view we knew that the Forest stretched above us, with all its untameable uplands. Perhaps because of this first view when it appeared so unattached, so solitary, so delicate in shape, I loved the Whimble more than all the other hills in the Forest. In the early morning or evening light, or when a slight mist lay over it, it resembled a mountain in a Japanese print. The boys had another reason for loving it, a reason that had nothing to do with its beauty. What fascinated them were the big slates that lay scattered on the top. These, they discovered, could be bowled down the steep side without danger, provided we first made a careful survey through binoculars to ensure that no sheep, or living soul, roamed below.

This was a thrilling game. No matter what the natural shape of the slates, as soon as we started to spin them they changed into cart-wheels that bounded down the hill and up into the air at a terrific pace. Sometimes one large slate would split into three or four smaller ones, and all would hop merrily along together. The amount of ground they covered before they lay flat and dead was amazing. Over the disused quarry they spun, over the scree, down the bare hillside and into a sea of heather, where their brief, rollicking life ended. We reckoned a first-class slate would travel 200 yards.

Looking back on our game now I wonder at times if we ought to have played it, but I am sure we never did any harm.

The view from the Whimble was glorious.

Great Cregiau, 2,000 feet, purple and green in summer time, reared cliff-like to the north. Dim shapes far to the south were the Brecon Beacons. Nearer at hand the Black Mountains dropped in dark terraces, and immediately below us lay a valley of surpassing greenness watered by the Summergill Brook. As I see it now, the sky seemed always piled high with bright clouds whose shadows changed perpetually in tint as they flew over bracken and heather and meadow-land. A little behind the Whimble a narrow valley, bounded by a stack of black rocks, gave out a wonderful echo. Whether because of delaying action by the wind I don't know, but always some two seconds passed before the response came with remarkable clearness. We called out whole sentences and they floated back word for word.

One day we went further in a north-westerly direction, dropped into a small valley where a brook splashed down a particularly stony bed, and climbed to a wide track of desolate boggy table-land. After all the variety and colour of the Whimble it looked black and sinister. No flowers except the dauntless little tormentil; not a bird to be seen though once we heard a raven's croak. Gladly we dropped to another valley further west where a golden-brown stream bore on its surface a host of scarlet rowan berries. We were in Harley Dingle. Suddenly the word 'Danger' in bold red letters gave us a nasty shock. Later we learned that this, the most beautiful valley in the Forest, was used at intervals for experimental work with machine-guns. This seemed to us abominable. But, when no rat-a-tat-tat sounded and no red flag flew, we went to it over and over again. You could always see ravens there, hear curlews and with luck find a dipper's nest. Ducks and geese populated the lower end, and the mill at the bottom gave generous teas.

An Expedition in the Forest with the Coracle

A year after we acquired the coracle Tom took in a resident patient named Mr. Jones, middle-aged, silent, inscrutable, who wanted to be kept off drink for a month. Usually, after long sessions in the surgery, Tom took him with him on his rounds, but one day when this was impossible he consigned him to my care.

'Keep the fellow amused and don't for heaven's sake let him go near a pub', he said. 'A single drink might start him off again'.

I felt the responsibility a bit overwhelming. What would be amusing but safe? An expedition to Radnor Forest would be *safe*, but would it appeal to urban Mr. Jones? How could it be made more amusing?

'Let's take the coracle!' cried Thomas, 'You've promised we should boat on a pool in the hills one day'.

Mr. Jones acquiesced without enthusiasm. The boys fixed the flat unwieldy craft on the back of the car and off we set. At Knighton we stopped to pick up meat-pies, buns, and bananas. Mr. Jones stared a little yearningly, I thought, at a group of hill farmers outside a pub, but made no attempt to join them. We took the road for Bleddfa and all went well till, as we rattled down one of the steep little hills, we heard ominous bumpings. The coracle was adrift and plunging wildly behind the car, held only by a single cord. Mr. Jones helped to tie her on again, but there were signs on his face of growing impatience. All our hands were very cold by the time we'd finished, and he muttered, 'What you want with that old thing beats me'.

At Pilleth, in an effort to interest him, I pointed out the field beside the Lugg where Owen Glendower fought a great battle and routed the English.

'An old man living here said that when he was a boy the rabbits were still digging up skulls', I pursued. He merely grunted. It's a beautiful field now, green and lawn-like, except for the hummocks near the river where many of the English dead are buried.

About two miles from Bleddfa we saw a track on our left that according to the map should bring us to a pool I had noted. We left the car and started off with the coracle, carrying her two at a time. She was unbelievably heavy and her great flat shape extremely awkward, especially as we were facing a rough wind and had over a mile to go.

Though I loved these hills I couldn't help now seeing them through Mr. Jones' eyes, as he walked in dogged silence. Certainly there was nothing to amuse him in the fawn-coloured grass bending before the wind, the little black bogs, the endless procession of low flying clouds.

'I hope this pool really exists,' he said.

I had begun to feel a bit anxious myself. We seemed to have walked miles. Supposing it had dried up or been drained !

But at last we saw it shining before us, backed by a sombre fir-wood. The boys gave a shout of triumph, took possession of the coracle and hurried ahead. By the time we caught them up they were already on the water.

I told Mr. Jones that I thought probably no one had paddled a coracle here since the time of the ancient Britons, or rather their Welsh equivalent.

He grunted again.

Our pool was quite a sizeable one, and the wind flurried it into tiny waves, and lumps of creamy foam. The boys, radiantly happy, shouted that they had found a wild duck's nest with ten eggs.

After a picnic in the lee of the wood, Mr. Jones decided that he would try a turn himself. I watched him set off with Thomas rather anxiously. If he fell in he would be sure to demand whisky at the first pub we came to. He insisted on using the paddle himself, with the oddest results. Though the coracle in the boys' hands and mine often took an erratic course it was nothing to what happened now. It spun round like a teetotum, to the sound of the boys' laughter and Mr. Jones' curses. Capsize seemed inevitable; the paddle beat the air, the boat, the water. Miraculously the pair returned safely to shore, driven by the wind. Mr. Jones looked damp, but proud and invigorated.

Mercifully, however, he did not want to try again. He went off for a stroll, the boys paddled about the pool with more laughter and shouts, but respected the neighbourhood of the duck's nest. I climbed up to the woods with my binoculars. When I got back and called to the boys that it was time to go home there was no sign of Mr. Jones.

We shouted in vain for ten minutes. Foreboding filled me. He had probably decided that a drink was essential after his trip in the coracle and had set off for the inn at Bleddfa. But when we got back to the car there he sat, smoking a cigarette and peacefully reading the newspaper. So I returned him to Tom unscathed. What he thought of our expedition we never knew. He was a man of few words.

A Discovery

One day two friends returned from an expedition with news of a small village they had found right within the bounds of Radnor Forest, and an inscription about witchcraft that had greatly interested them. At the first opportunity we set out to find it. A narrow lane seemed intent on taking us straight into the heart of the piled-up hills ahead, but after a couple of miles or so it brought us to the village. At the end of it stood a little white-washed church, with a half-timbered belfry tower and steeple built on a mound. Beside it grew a laden apple tree. Behind loomed a massive hill, and all round lay smooth, vivid meadows.

Once inside we made straight for the inscription on the wall, dated 1700, and rescued a few years ago from a rubbish heap. It concerned a certain Elizabeth Lloyd (or Looyd) who had either practiced witchcraft or been its victim. Written in English and dog Latin, it was a strange mixture of Paganism and Christianity. A priest named Hubert, evidently its author, asked in the name of the Trinity that the soul of this Elizabeth might be delivered 'from all evil spirits and from all evil men and women and wizards and hardness of heart'. An appeal to Christ to save her by 'the same power as he did cause the blind to see, the lame to walk and the dum to talk', was followed by a three-fold repetition of the Pater Noster, Ave Maria, and a further appeal to the Trinity, 'Adonay', and 'Tetragammaton'. An Abracadabra was set out in full triangular form at the end.

As we walked afterwards in the flowery meadows Elizabeth Lloyd was much in my mind, and I found myself trying to reconstruct the story of how Hubert, the village priest, had fought to rescue her from evil influences. When, on our way home, I learned in the village that the wife at the big farm would sometimes put up people for the night, we went to call on her, for I longed to spend more time here. We found a cheerful red-cheeked woman, and a daughter with mournful dark-grey eyes, in a cloud of chicken down. A pile of plucked birds were stacked on the table beside her. She was getting ready for Llandrindod Market, she said. Yes, she would take me for a couple of nights, if I didn't want any fancy cooking. I assured her my tastes were of the simplest. Did she know anything of Elizabeth Lloyd?

'Why yes, 'twas said she belonged to a farming family who still live round here, and that she'd fallen into the power of a real old witch—one of many who lived hereabouts in the old days'.

About a month later I went to stay two nights at the farm. After tea I strolled out in a thick, warm mist which made the trees and hedges look like cotton wool. Everything seemed larger than life, and the rocks beyond the village loomed huge and precipitous. Out of them flew a raven who croaked crossly at me. Muffled sounds drifted up—a sheep crying, a woman calling her ducks, a little owl in a ghostly tree.

Next day, Sunday, I attended a morning service, but my thoughts wandered away to Elizabeth Lloyd and Hubert the priest. Had he perhaps resembled the present parson, a breezy, horsey little man who would, surely, have dispelled the machinations of a witch with ease? When I talked to him later he told me that many of his parishioners still fell a prey to strange superstitions.

When I climbed Black Mixen—the dark mountain behind it— I understood better how the situation of the village, so remote, so dwarfed by the mountain's dark grandeur, would provide a fit breeding place for strange fears and fancies. A flaming sunset made the desolate boggy country at the top of the mountain both exciting and frightening, with its burning crimson and inky blackness. The little peat pools flashed fierily. Burnt furze bushes assumed strange shapes. Well, I thought, might an old witch have mumbled her charms and talked to the Devil up here. Fascinated, I lingered on so long that I had to make my way back down the mountain side in semi-darkness, and to slide much of the way on my behind for safety's sake.

Next day I set out with sandwiches for the lower lands. An unexpected splash drew me into a wood where I found a tiny stream turning a moss-grown water-wheel very languidly—only once in two minutes, because it was so small and the wheel so big.

Now I turned eastwards along a lane rich with autumn under the foot-hills, and reached a large farm beside a pond. On the gate, limp and draggled, hung a dead pole-cat. How I wished I could have seen it alive, for it must have once been such a handsome creature with its thick dark fur and primrose under-parts. A woman with a long, boney, horse-like face was drawing water from the pond. I tried to talk to her but she shook her head sadly. Evidently she was stone deaf.

Another big solid farmhouse beside a stream, Fossidoes by name, had clearly been the site of a castle. Beside it rose a massive ruined wall. In the lane nearby I met the first of several red squirrels. This one came running towards me with an acorn in its mouth. At sight of me it scampered up the nearest tree, glowering, stamping first its hind legs and then its front ones, arching and lashing its tail, and finally hanging upside down—all, I suppose, in the hope of intimidating me. Because of the acorn it couldn't chatter, but it succeeded in uttering a comical mewing. I left it in peace and went on up the hillside.

Returning by a different path I caught a glimpse of what seemed the ruins of a small church in an upland field, and cut across to explore. Yes, there was the roofless nave overgrown with elders, and full of sleepy birds, especially blackbirds, startled and vocal at this intrusion of their peace. Even when the little church stood whole and weather-proof the worshippers could scarcely have been more numerous than these blackbirds, for houses within reach were few indeed. I only wished I could have fallen in with some know-ledgeable old inhabitant to tell more about it. But never a soul appeared till I got back to my farm.

Next morning I visited the school because the mistress had invited me to come. Eighteen children, whom she taught single-handed, stood up and said 'Good morning'. Such a friendly, happy little lot. Many came on foot from lonely farms among the hills. Some were reading or writing, some sewing, some drawing. This mistress struck me as a remarkable woman; wise, humorous, loving her children and this countryside, to which she came a year ago from a town. I asked if I might return one day and take her for a drive. She assented with obvious pleasure.

I left the village more in love with it than ever. My only regrets centred round my kind hostess, and more particularly her daughter, pale-faced and sad. Watching them and talking to the mother I felt their life to be completely smothered in chicken feathers. This poultry business seemed the be-all and end-all of their existence. Evidently it brought in a lot of money, but at how great a cost. The look in the girl's eyes haunted me as I drove home. *She* never climbed the hills, nor saw the sunset from Black Mixen.

It was a good while before I had an opportunity—and excuse —to re-visit the village. It appeared that a patient of Tom's longed to see it again because as a girl she had been in service there and very happy. We had chosen one of those intoxicating May days that send your spirits soaring after a long wet spell. Bits of Wordsworth kept coming into my head as we drove along the little switch-backed, hair-pin-bended road to the Forest. There really was extra radiance in the grass. Curlews certainly filled the air with 'joyous sound', and young lambs bounded about in the fields, and often across the road. And when we reached the village the fields were flowerier than ever, and the little white steeple seen against its mountain background even more attractive than before. While my passenger chatted with her old friends I went to the school and planned an expedition with the teacher. At the farm I found my late hostess suffering from high blood pressure. The colour in her cheeks had faded, so had the energy, that she used to radiate. There were still chickens on the table but not so many as before. I only caught a fleeting glimpse of the daughter, seemingly more dispirited than ever. I felt terribly sorry for them both.

As we drove home my companion told me a story of her days in the village that we had just left behind. When she worked there a pretty young farmer's daughter was to be married at Easter. But a little time before the wedding-day she fell mysteriously ill, pined rapidly, and died. Now this poor young lady had been in the habit of continually nibbling the wheat as she fed it to the hens.

' "You shouldna do that", everyone told her, but she couldna bear to give up the habit and when they held an inquest on her they found corn growing green inside her'.

That was my friend's story, but Tom firmly refused to believe it.

Water-Break-Its-Neck

Water-Break-Its-Neck was a thrilling, beautiful place, and the one in the Forest we visited most often. When special visitors stayed with us, we always said, 'You *must* see Water-Break-Its-Neck'.

At the first opportunity after we noticed the name on the map we set off to find it. A small stream, two miles or so out of the trim little town of New Radnor, led us past a massive farmhouse, that looked as if it had been once fortified, into a wood where immensely tall fir trees grew. We followed the stony course of our little stream round several bends, under rocky cliffs that grew taller and taller; here the firs gave place to birch, rowans and oaks, and the rocks were festooned with ivy. Suddenly a pleasing roar of water filled our ears and there before us was this splendid fall, tumbling down a precipitous wall of rock into a pool, and half veiling itself in spray. We adopted it straight away. Not only was it a desirable place in its own right, but it gave the boys an inspiration. Here, under this mighty waterfall we would launch some gay celluloid ducks they had recently acquired, and race them right down the stream till it joined the Summergill Brook in the valley.

The idea was a huge success, though, because the bed of the stream was too stony at its source we started the ducks a little lower down. I am almost ashamed to say how often after this we drove to Water-Break-Its-Neck for a duck-race, nor can I attempt to estimate how many ducks got lost in water-holes, and this in spite of the long bamboos we carried. Perhaps some are still slowly disintegrating to this very day. But, with or without ducks, Water-Break-Its-Neck, at all seasons, and more especially after heavy rains, remained among our best loved haunts.

One of the guests we took there was a little Basque refugee. It was on a January day when the ravine was all black and white, red and dark green. Dark shining masses of ivy flowed down the cliffs and crimson dogwood bent over the bed of the stream. Beyond the trees the white sheet of water swept over its wall of dark rock in truly break-neck fashion, roaring deliciously. Little Maria stood entranced, unable to take her eyes off it. She had never seen a waterfall before.

I have forebodings that now the gorge may be more overgrown and less approachable, and that some of the water pouring down to swell the fall may be drawn off higher up and have diminished its volume. But I shall always remember Water-Break-Its-Neck as it first burst into view over forty years ago, and the line of ducks, red, blue, yellow, green, bobbing along the stream below it.

Maesmelan

No account of Radnor Forest as we knew it would be complete without Maesmelan. I came to it by chance because of a B.B.C. enquiry about what feature of their programmes country women enjoyed most. My job was to visit a few of the more remote houses.

After I had sought help from my schoolmistress friend, I struggled up lanes full of holes and enormous puddles on the fringes of the Forest; met one woman who said her day was made when Frank Phillips—'him with the golden voice'—wished her good morning; another, a serious-minded young mother, who wanted more talks about children and education; another who never tired of hymn-singing. Finally, I came to a long low white farm on the banks of the Summergill Brook, called Maesmelan. In the yard I fell in with a man I'd met during a prolonged drought, when he told me how he changed his boots three times a day because of the hardness of the ground. He gave me a friendly welcome and took me in to his wife and daughter in a big old-fashioned kitchen. We sat beside the fire for a long, rewarding talk. The wife was dark, stout, determined-looking; a staunch Liberal, with extremely strong views on the international situation. She burned with sympathy for Spain and Czechoslovakia, and had no patience with Chamberlain and his lot. Talks on foreign affairs were the breath of life to her. Also brass bands. Her daughter, Margaret, aged sixteen, who had just left school, loved country and natural history talks, lively music, and talks about books. She was an omnivorous reader, but her mother declared some of those from the school library are 'disgusting', and she made me promise to send her a list of really good ones for her daughter. Also particulars of the Duchess of Atholl's knitting competition in aid of Spanish refugees.

That was the first of many visits. Whether by myself, with Jill, with friends, I could always be sure of a welcome at all seasons, at any time of day—sure, too, of lively talk and exchange of ideas.

Sometimes the Summergill, running at the bottom of the field, was a true summer stream, gentle and flower-bordered. Sometimes, the swollen springs from the surrounding hills changed it to a torrent, bearing along islands of water-weeds, and sometimes a water-bird's nest. A moorhen sat gallantly on her eggs as she was swept away.

The farmer would be kept busy driving up his sheep from the flooded meadows to the safety of the yard. Maesmelan, so good in itself, further served as a jumping off ground for desirable places such as Cym-y-bout and Black Yatt, over the hills to the south.

Once or twice I stayed for a night or two, and coming home in semi-darkness from a long walk was guided first by the shape of the Mynd standing black against the sky, behind the farm, and then as I drew nearer, by a light shining from the window of the ghostly white house.

Caer Caradoc

Though the Long Mynd is a splendid and immensely popular hill, we loved Caer Caradoc, on the opposite side of the Stretton Valley, better, partly perhaps because its southern slopes gave us our first Shropshire resting place. *Then* a terrific thunderstorm had driven us down to the valley, and henceforward the rather wild weather in which we chose to visit it helped to accentuate its uncompromising character.

It was on a January day, after heavy rainfalls, that we left the car near a great stone called the Gaer Stone and set off over squelching fields.

At the foot of the ridge an old woman, a young one, and two boys were picking up sticks, in clothes that seemed planned to match the landscape. The old woman wore a faded purple blouse and a sacking apron, the younger, a coat and hat of tawny brown. They smiled at us as we made our way cautiously and the girl said, 'You hunna mind if your shoes be wet for a week.'

It was a true forecast, but when we reached the top we felt it had been worth the hard wet climb. Across the valley the Long Mynd was purple, to the south-east Wenlock Edge blue as juniper berries, the lower sky pale and luminous, topped by a long straight-edged inky cloud like a half-lowered blind. The wind blew rough and cold, and when we'd found the rather too tidied-up cave of Caractacus (whom the historians have removed from this hill that suits him so well) we were glad to drop into a little hollow and eat our bread and cheese. Here we watched that ominous cloud letting loose a flying grey rain-storm over Wenlock Edge, while we sat serene and untouched. After climbing every possible rock and marching round the big Iron-Age camp, we started home.

Caradoc, towering behind, seemed a huge sleeping beast, ox-like first but turning into a sea-lion. As we hurried through the twilight we passed the most desolate and lonely little farm I've ever met with in this country of lonely farms. Not only did the dark hills dominate it behind, but a tall dense evergreen pressed up close to the door and surely shut out every vestige of light from the two narrow windows. An unkempt garden plot was littered with old iron and dilapidated sheds. A sea of mud, where a few melancholy hens moved listlessly, surrounded it. No other sign of life appeared. What kind of people lived here and how did they endure the wild winter months, we wondered? But we did not summon up courage to knock at the door. Darkness was falling rapidly and anyway we felt we'd be unwelcome.

Our next visit was when, during the Christmas holidays, we woke to a roaring west wind.

I said, 'Where's the most exciting place to go and meet it?' and the boys said, 'Caer Caradoc.'

So off we went. The gale grew more and more terrific as we climbed, and when we reached the top Oliver was blown backwards. Our handkerchiefs were torn from our pockets and sailed away over the hills. The clouds marched steadily overhead in a dark army. The ones scurrying in front were little ragged soldiers, and the big ones lumbering behind, the machine-guns and armoured cars.

It was hard to breathe, let alone speak, when we faced it on the downward journey. We arrived home elated and ravenously hungry.

Under Brown Clee

On a soft warm January day, the world flooded with sunshine, we drove through Corve Dale in search of an ancient little church called The Heath. Having missed our road out of Diddlebury we eventually turned off along a twisty lane to the village of Holdgate. A church with a fortress-like tower stood on a high ridge, but when—armed with a massive key that hung in the porch—we tried to enter we were completely frustrated. We each fought with that key in turn, until, exhausted, we left the church to look for the remains of a castle in a neighbouring farmyard.

Here we were met by the farmer, a tall, burly, red-faced person, who said, Yes, there was a bit of the castle to be seen at the back of his house, and the tickets would be half-a-crown for each of us. I looked rather askance at this, but taking courage from the twinkle in his eye, we waded ankle-deep in mud, and free of charge, to the back premises and found a ruined round tower with steep-pitched roof, against which the rest of the house had been built.

At the church we struggled again with the key, and had just succeeded in bursting it open—a literal burst which shot us all head-long forward—when there stood our farmer, come to see if we needed help. As church-warden he felt it right to show us round. Under his guidance we admired the ancient font and the four strange creatures who supported it, and the misericord carved with a dragon and another odd beast, and the old black oak box-pews.

'But not many sits in 'em now', he said. We asked if a squire occupied the front one?

'No', he answered with relish, 'Thank the Lord. Them that sat —rarely mark you—in that pew, sold their property and took theirselves off, and good riddance too. They'd never done aught but draw money from the people of Holdgate and spend it in London'. Then he heaved a great sigh, and spoke of hard times, and as we parted I felt constrained to put a shilling in his hand—my only coin—which he accepted without protest.

From Holdgate a winding lane led us to a hamlet that seemed literally at the end of the world. It lay in a little dip of the hills with a steep shoulder rising straight behind it, and it consisted of two or three cottages and a mill with a wheel—stationary for the moment—turned by a stream that came frolicking down the hillside. The miller, who sat in the sun on a low wall, told us that this was Bouldon, and that few people were as venturesome as ourselves. No wonder; the road out must have been among the worst in England. Following his directions, we came to a stony, precipitous lane and so at last to the Heath—a little early Norman church standing by itself in a field.

The weather-beaten walls were golden brown, the design of the simplest, without tower or steeple. The key had to be fetched from a farm about 300 yards away, and again we struggled with an obstinate lock. Clearly the locksmiths in these parts had resolved to make entry dauntingly difficult. Again we each tried; then hot and tired we sat down on the steps to eat our lunch. Fortified, we renewed the battle—but in vain. Finally a young man passing along the road, burst it open after several violent wrenches. Yes, he admitted, it was a terrible stubborn lock and he'd heard tell that many visitors went away disappointed.

We felt grateful that we were not among them, for it was a most rewarding place. No aisles; lancet windows of clear glass, narrow and deeply set; pews of dark oak; a roof of rough beams; no disfiguring tablets on the white-washed walls. I found it easy to pray in this place.

From the Heath, we wound close under Brown Clee to Clee St. Margaret, where the churchyard was full of the graves of Millichopes and snowdrops.

Our road now climbed so violently that I thought it was determined to take us to the top of the Brown Clee, towering gaunt and bare above us. But it changed its mind and dropped us safely back into Stoke Milborough.

I explored this country under Brown Clee a second time in March with Mrs. Mac.

We turned off at Diddlebury to Tugford and Abdon—a loveable village right under the hill, with a winding street and an old grey stone house festooned with two big wreaths of ivy. In the middle of the village a stream wandered off down a lane. We had a picnic tea looking up at Abdon Burf, a remarkable British earthwork standing at nearly 1,800 feet. My feet ached to be up it, but time was too short. We drove along banks thick with such a wealth of white violets as I'd never seen before. The whole air was sweet with them.

At Stoke St. Milborough we found a Holy well dedicated to St. Milburga, daughter of Penda, pagan King of Mercia. She seems not only to have been a saint, but a most practical and able one who ruled her nunnery at Wenlock and all its wide lands with wisdom and foresight. Her Well is fed by a spring that leaps straight from the bank in a surprising fashion. These villages under the Clee are rich in similar lively springs. As I drank at it, I told a passer-by I thought she lived in a most beautiful place.

'Well', she answered. 'We don't think about it much, and then, when we've been away and come back, we always say we haven't seen nowhere no nicer!'

On the Stiperstones

Sometimes we passed under Shropshire's wildest hills, the Stiperstones, on our way to Shrewsbury; sometimes we saw their rocky crowns, over 1,700 feet at their highest point, from miles away. Always our feet ached to climb them. At last, after a drenching summer, we set off on a misty September day, turned up a side-road that led past old lead-mines first worked in the time of Hadrian, and left our car on a forlorn bit of country called The Bog. Then we waded up through bracken and mist, which suddenly broke to reveal the rugged piles of rock above us. In the wavering light they resembled huge crouching beasts, and detached rocks took on uncanny shapes. It seemed easy now to understand how, long after he resisted the Normans, the British Chieftain, Wild Edric, was seen galloping with his train over these hills whenever war was in the air.

Close by, as we climbed, a patient-faced farmer was raking together his sodden hay, with a dejected cow and her calf to keep him company. A more cheerful touch was a line of ducks waddling through the bright green grass. They obviously had a sense of pattern, for first came a white one, then a black one, and so on till the sixth. The man spoke of the vile summer with sad resignation, but no bitterness. He had learned to take whatever came to him.

Up the steep slopes we plodded through heather, through furze bushes, through whinberries. Among them grew an unfamiliar little plant with shining dark leaves, scarlet berries, and a few white or pale pink waxen flowers. Could they be cowberries, otherwise small cranberries, I wondered?

A woman busy picking them into a tin can said, 'Yes, we picks 'em every year and bottles 'em in cold water. They keeps beautiful all through the winter. Thirty year I've been at it'. She pointed out a little grey stone house tucked under the nearest peak and said it was her home. To leave it and all her bothers behind and come berry-picking was always a treat. We too began to pick the berries into a paper-bag. But not for long. The boys' legs itched to climb the rocks piled above us. They dashed up each one in turn, including the great Devil's Chain, I following more sedately.

112

At a hospitable-looking cottage, where a bush of Lad's Love grew by the door and a churn and butter-hands dried on the hedge, a rosy-cheeked young woman promised us tea if we'd return in half-an-hour. So we made off for a solitary rock called the Nipstone, and on the way passed a ruined homestead. You could trace each room by the heaped-up stones among the heather, but it was the garden that enchanted me.

Where flowers and vegetables had once grown spread a square of velvety grass, surrounded by a low bank, planted with laburnums, a lilac, a damson, and small willow trees. The little lawn, completely hemmed in by them, looked so secret, so delicate, that to put foot on it would have seemed sacrilege. I thought how lovely it would be to build up the house again and come to it when the mood called you and circumstances permitted. The only crab was that forlorn, half-deserted little village called The Bog just below.

When they'd climbed the Nipstone, the boys dragged out an old truck lying beside a deserted mine, and had a few mad rides down the hillside. Then back to the good tea waiting for us. As we ate the young woman talked in the friendliest, frankest way. Her husband had been employed in the last lead mine worked at The Bog, but was now on the dole. They kept a cow, a few sheep and grew a bit of corn, but the soil was poor. However, she appeared absolutely happy and declared she never found time heavy on her hands. Lately several people had asked for tea, and it was all because of that woman called Mary Webb. But she didn't believe she wrote all those books. 'Why not?' I asked. 'Because she'd been dead for years, yet she wrote of the death of an old man who only died three years ago. That proved it, didn't it?'

In the chimney corner hung a finely chased copper powder-flask that had belonged to her husband's father. Her husband was very proud of it, and liked it well polished. A handsome oak corner-cupboard lined with mahogany hung on the wall, and there was an old oak bureau too. She, like her husband, was proud of these things, but she didn't hesitate to voice her preference for modern furniture. I feared she would fall an easy prey to some acquisitive and persuasive collector one day.

There were lots of red squirrels, she told us, in the firwood above the house, and many foxes on the hills. One of them always reared her young under the Nipstone. It was a pleasure to look at her as well as talk to her. She had such rosy, dimpled cheeks.

I was glad I had the memory of her and of our good tea as we steered ourselves back to the car through a bog in thick drizzle. When we looked back the whole Stiperstone ridge was completely blotted out, and the landscape immensely desolate. It was a wild and splendid bit of country, but not many people could have accepted it as a home either with the resignation of the farmer raking his hay, or the cheerfulness of the young woman.

On Kerry Hill in Summer

Not till the September after we settled in Shropshire did we get to Kerry Hill—the high hill we had often looked at far away to the north-west beyond the source of the Clun. Since it cradled three rivers—the Teme, the Mule and the Ithon—we felt confident of good exploring. A house named the Cider House on our map also sounded enticing.

After zig-zagging two or three miles above the Anchor, we left the car at the highest point, and struck south-west along a grass track. Though a dark cloud hid the Welsh mountains the view was grand. A deep purple shadow rested on the nearer hills, and above them lay a bank of pearly cloud. A fresh breeze blew in our faces. We felt we could have walked forever, here, on top of the world, as it seemed. Now and then we passed a little rushy pool, haunt of dragon flies. One was blue-and-gold, another, bronze—so enormous that for a moment we mistook it for a little bird.

Away to the south a small valley cutting into the heart of the hill suggested the source of the Teme.

We had just finished our bread-and-cheese, when a man with a face like a full moon, on a pony as stout as himself, pointed out the way to the Cider House. There, we thought with satisfaction, we would get a good drink later on. But as it was still early afternoon, we turned off beside a pinewood and dropped suddenly into a little ravine where a lively stream splashed down in small waterfalls between rocks blazing with gorse and heather. This we decided was the Ithon, but later found it to be a distinguished tributary.

Now we turned, warm, exhilarated, thirsty, hopeful, towards the Cider House; a small, white-washed building standing among some trees in a flagged yard. There seemed nobody about. Nobody answered our knock. A tortoise-shell cat, sunning himself on a wall, watched us disdainfully. The Cider House clearly would provide neither cider *nor* tea. What made it still more annoying was the way that moon-faced man had given no hint of what awaited us. Sadly we turned away. Throughout the expedition the thought of the Cider House had shone for us like a beacon, and this silence, this emptiness, was a cruel blow. But in the end we met with a hospitality that richly compensated us.

We had dropped down to the west of another young river, clearly the Mule, burrowing its way out of a deep cleft, when we saw a farmhouse at the head of a wooded dingle. We made straight for it. Other creatures besides ourselves also were seeking refreshment. Two men stopped reaping an oat-field above us and started towards the farm. A flock of geese with out-stretched necks scurried across the pasture, and a number of pigs and a few hens were also on the run. One of the men, evidently the farmer himself, met us when we reached the gate.

'Tea?' he said, 'Why, to be sure', and he called to his daughter (his wife, he told us, was dead). Smiling, she led us into the kitchen —a wonderful kitchen, paved with red-and-black tiles scrubbed so that no speck of dirt showed on them, and the furniture all shone as brightly as their brass handles.

As for the daughter, she looked as though she'd just stepped from her bath. She had a clear delicate skin, shy brown eyes, and smooth silky hair drawn into a bun. Her father put more sticks on the fire, the kettle boiled and soon we sat down to home-made bread (twelve large loaves a week, she made, she said), butter, whinberry jam, and cake. The two chattered away with no touch of stiffness, though the farmer refused to sit down at the table until we'd finished no matter how hard we tried to make him. He had lived here for fifty-five years. He was churchwarden, his daughter played the organ. Their vicar was a bachelor but everyone wished he'd marry. There was never anything going on in their village but whist-drives and dances. A worse summer he couldn't remember. He thought nothing of Craven Arms Sheep Fair, though the folk there fancied it something tremendous. But the Kerry Fair—that was truly a grand affair, and the Kerry sheep with their speckled white faces, the prettiest of all sheep—far superior to the Clun Forest ones. We asked about the Cider House. It had never been a licensed house, he said, but in former days cider could be sold without a licence, and the people living there brewed it, and folk from all around came to buy it, so good it was. Nothing to touch it was made now-a-days.

Full of tea and bread-and-butter and country talk, we said a grateful good-bye. They would take no payment. The farmer walked with us a little way to point out our path past a place called Hangman's House. On a tree up there a man had been hanged for stealing a horse. There might be a few stones of the old house still left.

Back on Kerry Hill the haze over the Welsh hills had finally melted and under a clear apricot sky the horns of Cader Idris stood up firmly. Then, even as we looked, a faint luminous peak, pink as a dog-rose took shape in the far north. We had seen Snowdon.

Kerry Hill in a snow storm

One January morning I woke to find a light powdering of snow and a promise of more to come. So I suggested to the boys that we should drive to Kerry Hill and see how the Welsh mountains looked in winter. Oliver thought it a good idea, but Thomas a silly one. 'Well then, stay at home', I said. But he wouldn't. Extremely cross he still insisted on coming.

The landscape grew whiter the higher we went, and we reached Kerry Hill in a snowstorm. Thomas continued to look both cross and miserable. He thought I'd seen how foolish was this expedition and that we would now drive straight home. That was not my idea, and by the time we had eaten our sandwiches in the car we sat in a blaze of sunshine. But further away low indigo clouds hid much of the wide tumble of hills before us. Arrows of light shot out and rested for a moment on first one mountain top and then another. The pine-woods nearby were coal-black against all the whiteness.

My last sandwich swallowed, I set off for a quick walk, but Thomas remained huddled in the back of the car and Oliver stayed to keep him company. Far away to the west a huge grey cloud came flying towards me, but I reckoned it had a long way to travel before it would actually reach me. Its dark wings spread wider and wider like some gigantic hawk. Suddenly a few flakes of snow swirled about me, and in a moment that relentless cloud enveloped me in a dense snowstorm. The boys watched gleefully as I struggled back to the car, and hoped I'd show signs of discomfort. To their disappointment I didn't—partly due to pride and partly to a fierce delight in having faced the elements.

116

I drove very slowly through the snow down the long hill. Thomas relapsed into morose silence. When we reached home he said 'I don't feel well'.

I thought he was trying to make me sorry about the expedition. However, when I took his temperature it was 101°. This filled him with satisfaction and me with remorse. 'I felt bad before we started', he said as I tucked him up in bed after a hot drink.

'Then why on earth not have said so?'

'I didn't want to be left behind'.

'You're a ridiculous boy. Now go to sleep'.

He smiled and his eyes had closed before I left the room. He felt he had justified himself, and when my mild remorse was over I was able to draw a strange pleasure from the memory of that great snow-laden cloud flying straight at me over the hills.

Over Plynlimon

When we had climbed most of the hills within thirty miles or so the dark mass of Plynlimon as seen from the top of Kerry Hill challenged us, not only for its own sake but because it cradled the Wye, and exploring sources was a special passion of mine.

So one day in mid-September off we set in the car with knapsacks, resolved to cross the mountain and to stay the night at a small village on the further side. This village, according to our map was called Dylife.

Over the hills to Knighton, through Llanidloes and Llangurig, we went, and finally left our car at a wayside garage near a tributary of the Wye, a fine lively stream in its own right. We would follow it to the top of Plynlimon and then find the Wye.

Unfortunately the sky grew dark and threatening as we climbed, and when we reached the place where our stream oozed from a bog, I realised that time and weather alike were against us. The day was half over. The source of the Wye must keep its secret. We must set our noses for Dylife.

Never had I been in a sadder more uncompromising bit of country than the one that faced us now. This mountain, that had looked mysterious and inviting from a distance, consisted of huge expanses of rough, boggy land, of yellow grass, of deep black gullies. As we crossed one of these it occurred to me it must actually be the source of the Severn, but I dared not turn aside. There was not a flower, not a bird to cheer us, till a scatter of sweet cries overhead revealed a flock of golden plover.

On the long downward drop the sight of deserted mines ahead filled me with foreboding, and my worst fears were confirmed as we drew near what I had pictured as a kindly little village. The black mouths of deserted houses gaped at us, and the only sound building was a small sombre inn. Dylife had evidently died with its mines. Beggars can't be choosers. I knocked uneasily at the inn door. After a long pause a repellant old woman thrust her face out at us. It was covered with spots. Her eyes were a sour green, her teeth horribly decayed. We agreed afterwards that she looked like an old witch, and a nasty one at that.

In answer to my request for beds for the night she spat out, 'No room here', and slammed the door in our faces, but not before a horrid smell from the darkness behind her reached us. We felt deep relief. Far better sleep on the cold hillside than enter that God-forsaken house. As we made our way haltingly along the twilit deserted road we met a country man whose healthy, good-humoured face shone like a burst of sunshine after the old hag's.

'Cut off across the moor yonder, for about two miles', he told us, 'and you'll come to a house where they'll take you in, I shouldn't wonder'.

We set off by a vague path through the heather with darkness slipping deeper round us every moment. No house appeared and probably never would. The boys grew sadly silent. Suddenly a light shone out—never in my life a more welcome one. We felt like benighted travellers in a fairy-tale.

Thomas bravely hurried ahead, only to be checked by the barking of a dog, who rushed out to meet him. He was nervous of dogs at any time, and Welsh dogs attached to lonely houses can be the very devil. He stood hesitating.

Then came the reassuring sound of a woman's voice calling back the dog. The three of us walked anxiously towards the open door where she stood framed in the lamplight.

Her vivid dark eyes gazed at us in amazement.

'Come you in', she said.

In no time at all we were seated round a blazing wood fire and being fed on eggs and bread-and-butter and cocoa. After all our disappointment over that little ruined village, our anxiety, our tiredness, it seemed almost too good to be true.

118

The husband and wife and bright-eyed daughter, typical of the very best Welsh country people, sat watching us and asking questions They clucked their tongues when we spoke of the inn, and looked meaningfully at each other. The daughter then hurried off to make our beds.

I was too tired to be haunted that night by the old witch and the dark lonely moor and so were the boys. Deep delicious sleep wrapped us round till the girl called us to a breakfast of porridge and eggs-and-bacon. When the time came to leave we were handed a bill for ten shillings for the three of us. Only with difficulty did I persuade our hostess to accept double.

'What do you call this place?' I asked.

Surely, I thought, we'll come here again one day.

'Stay-a-little', I understood her to say. Such a wonderfully suitable name. It was only later I found it to be 'Stay Little'. The dropping of the 'a' made all the difference to the name, but for us it always remained a house which had welcomed us and saved us from a night in the heather.

The rain that had threatened all the previous day began in earnest when we had scarcely gone a mile on our homeward journey and never stopped again. Anyone who has walked on Plynlimon in bad weather will know what rain can be up there. But once we were soaked to the skin it didn't seem to matter too much. And there was one bright spot; the discovery of a patch of cloud-berries—beautiful apricot cloud-berries—so beautiful that it seemed almost a crime to eat them. But we made short work of them all the same. When we finally settled our wet bodies into the car the boys said, 'We really did cross Plynlimon'. They forgot about the Wye, and I remembered Stay-a-little.

A Ridiculous Walk

This walk illustrates the danger when two strong-willed women, each intent on her own line, walk together. M. and I, after a visit to a friend in his entirely delightful, entirely unusual, little house above Beguildy, stayed the night at the inn.

Next morning we set off with our knapsacks to cross the Beacon and stay at Llangunllo. Somehow we missed the proper path, and at once began to quarrel about the right line. The result—an absurd compromise whereby I sometimes accepted her way, and she mine.

When we had left the Beacon behind us and come down into a small valley feeling completely lost, we decided to go to the only house we saw and ask for directions. A kindly farmer asked us in and gave us large mugs of his home-made perry. For me, at all events, this proved fatal. I sat back in my comfortable chair sipping the perry, and watching M., who looked very intelligent and wide-awake, listening as our host told her how to get to Llangunllo. Needless to say we were, at the moment, completely off-line.

How nice, I thought, that I needn't listen to all this 'turn left, turn right' stuff. Grateful and much refreshed off we started again, I, for once, ready to follow my companion obediently when she turned right outside the gate. After two or three miles the lie of the land made me sure something was wrong. This was confirmed by a road-man who told us to go back the way we had come. When we started off from the farm we should have turned *left*, he told us. My re-crimination was mild because I'd been too lazy to listen. Now we had walked a good six miles for nothing. Off we set again, very silent, and hoping that our late host would not see us as we passed his gate. To our relief there was no sign of him.

After a good while it grew excessively warm in our little shut-in-lane, and I said I really must sit down.

'No', said M. emphatically, 'that would be fatal. We must keep going'.

I persisted that I would rest for five minutes, and then follow her. Off she went without a word. I crossed the road for a better seat, and that was my undoing. Still perhaps a little bedazed by the perry, and also by the warmth of the sun, I got up, shouldered my knapsack and set out at a good pace. But that wretch M. had clearly gone at a still better one. At each bend of the lane I expected to see her striding along but never did. Resentfully I thought, 'If I'd been in her place I'd have waited'.

Gradually horrid doubts filled me. Surely this lane was familiar? But then all these lanes look alike, I told myself. I slogged on. Then suddenly I saw our farmhouse gate for the *third* time. I tried to assure myself this was impossible. But, misery, it proved all too true. I had forgotten the fatal crossing of one side of the road for the other, and once again had been walking in exactly the wrong direction.

I won't enlarge on what happened after that. It was already dark. All hope of reaching Llangunllo was over. By a strange and devious route that I can never explain I found myself, cross, sad, back at the inn from which we had started so blithely that morning.

The inn-keeper, who found it hard to restrain his smiles, agreed to put me up for a second night. As soon as I could pull myself together I telephoned to the only inn at Llangunllo.

Yes, came the answer, my friend had arrived but had gone to the police to tell them that I was missing and she feared I was lost among the hills. Five minutes later she herself rang me up, too breathless with relief for any reproaches.

'They were just setting off with a rug and brandy to find you', she said.

The end of it was that her sister drove post-haste from Kington to fetch first her and then me to stay the night in luxury—a happy ending to a ridiculous story.

IX

BESIDE THREE RIVERS

Beside the Onny

My first acquaintance with the Onny began when, soon after our arrival in Shropshire, I accompanied Tom for a visit to a cottage near Horderley, just above the little railway line from Craven Arms to Church Stretton. It is a bigger river than our Brook, and winds between steeper and more wooded banks. High up one of these, hidden among the trees, stood the cottage. As I sat waiting for him down on the road, a strong, familiar scent reached me. What was it? Bog myrtle of course. I found it in the undergrowth. This scent helped me to locate the cottage again when I was asked to drop a bottle of medicine there a little later. Jill went with me and we drove slowly along above the river, sniffing the air as we went. Suddenly there it was again, strong and sweet.

I left Jill in the car and climbed up through the trees, but when I returned the wretch had taken herself off and was trotting as fast as her short legs would carry her towards the level crossing at Horderley Station. She had evidently heard a train approaching and hoped to be in time to watch it. I shouted in vain, and then in a panic began to run myself. But I soon realised there was no cause for anxiety. The funny little train came puffing gently along as though it had eternity before it, and in front of it ran six hens. That was the dearest little railway I ever met, and it passed through a rare bit of country, the Onny on one side and the Long Mynd rising, fold on fold, above it.

The next time I went to the Onny was in search of a party of cloggers, who, so Harry said, were working near Plowden. Ever since I heard of the clogs swept away by a flood I had wanted to see cloggers at work. But no longer, it seemed, did they come to our Brook.

On a cold but pleasant February day I set out on my bicycle for Plowden Station, where a waggoner told me that I would find the

122

cloggers a mile away up the river, in one of those 'dumbledy' (hummocky) fields. Close by a man was harrowing with a handsome pair of horses, one cream, one black. They seemed in a skittish mood, and he had to trot to keep up with them. The Long Mynd, sometimes so dark and sombre, today was as delicately-tinted as a pigeon's breast. The subdued pink of dead bracken, the green and ashen grey of the hillside, faded imperceptibly into one another and over all hung a faint bloom. Apricot-coloured chips heaped on the river bank, and a man driving by with sacks full of them, showed me I was approaching the cloggers.

A 'dumbledy' field appeared on my left, and a cloud of blue smoke drifted up among the trees. I left my cycle beside a gate, went through and found a clogger at work in an open-ended tent of ancient sacking stretched over a rough timber framework supported by a long upright pole. Outside a fire of chips and brushwood crackled. He was weather-beaten and wiry, with a tuft of dark hair rearing from his bald forehead, a tan shirt, dark trousers and gum-boots, and a friendly grin. I sat down on a stump to watch him shape with his big knife four clogs—three for a man and one for a child. The knife was rigged up on short wooden legs, and powerful leverage was gained by a hook and bolt at one end. He could make about thirty to forty dozen clogs a week, and was paid one-and-six a dozen. Out of this he first must pay for the wood to be sawn into logs. Not a lot of money, but he seemed well content. There wouldn't be many of his sort left soon, he said. Clogs were largely made in factories now, but they didn't last so long, and they let the wet through more easily. He stopped frequently to unhook the knife and rub it on a thick leather shield strapped round his left thigh.

Finally he tossed me a clog and told me to pull off my gloves and feel the greater smoothness after the knife had just been leathered and pointed out how remarkably the graining of the wood resembled the shape of the human foot. There was no wood like alder for clogs. It came away clean as butter.

As it was growing late reluctantly I left him in his tent under the trees, intent on his work, but not too intent to call out:

'You can come again if you've a mind.'

Harrowing was still going on in the big field, but the horses had lost their sprightliness and moved soberly with bowed heads as I cycled home in the twilight.

When I managed a second visit in the autumn the cloggers had gone, never, I believe, to return. Are there any left now in England, I wonder? Most unlikely, I fear.

But I made many other expeditions to the Onny, for it is the prettiest of all the rivers round here, except of course our Brook. Steep wooded hills rise above it on one side, and on the other vivid green fields lie between it and the Long Mynd.

One October afternoon lingers in my mind. A bush of maple, leaning over a pool, seemed carved in gold against the dark water, and a clump of bronzed fern glowed nearby. Suddenly out shot a kingfisher, who proceeded to play a game with me. He would flash ahead till the next bend, hide, re-appear, speed low over the water, hide again, re-emerge. Six times to my delight he repeated this performance. Then with a gay cry of triumph he flew back the way he had come. Above me the Long Mynd was again many-coloured. From a little grey home, guarded by two Scots firs, on the hillside, a woman came out and stood there with the low sunlight making a halo round her head.

But I remember the Onny best, when, after weeks of frost and snow, I heard as I approached, strange noises—banging, rattling, groaning noises, and found that my gentle river was bearing down huge blocks of ice which jostled against each other as they were swept along the dark water. I felt as if I had walked straight into one of those Russian stories that describe the coming of Spring.

Beside the Lugg

From the day that I found its source in haphazard manner, I felt a warm affection for the Lugg.

The children were away, and I had promised myself a long quiet day on the hills beyond Knighton and, though it was raining when I started, go I would. My faith seemed justified. As I drew up at a farm at the end of a lane west of Knucklas the sun came out, and after one light shower it shone the whole day. The farm seemed deserted. I left my car in the yard and climbed a steep lane to a fine bare ridge. Below on my left lay a little green valley, peaceful and empty—just a small grey farm here and there beside the stream. From a rocky crag a buzzard soared and once I heard the croak of a raven. A turn westwards for two or three miles up-hill brought me to a delicious pool in the heather, where swam a brood of baby ducklings, untroubled by my intrusion. Not so their mother. She repeatedly landed in front of me and did her utmost to lure me away with a pretended broken wing. Hard-heartedly I didn't play up, so she returned and admonished her family to beware of the sinister figure on the bank. They listened indifferently and continued to dart about after small fry.

It was then, just below the pool, that I found I had reached the source of the Lugg. There are few more rewarding things than the unexpected discovery of a river's source. At first this was the merest trickle, enough to give a low gurgle now and then. But in no time it changed to a dashing stream that went singing southwards down the hill. Ponies frolicked and sheep grazed wherever a bit of grass showed itself amid the heather. After a mile or so the baby Lugg was joined by another lively infant stream—so lively that I felt obliged to turn aside and look at all its little waterfalls. Here grew delicate pale rosettes of butterwort leaves, each a shining green star-fish set among the stones. No blossom yet, but one or two buds.

On I went down the main stream till I reached a really big waterfall, where I paddled in a pool below. I longed to go with my river right down into the valley, but thought better of it when I remembered the two hours walking between me and the car. But I resolved to return with the boys as soon as might be. During my whole day on the hills from 12 p.m. to 6 p.m. I saw not a single human being except a man on a pony far away in the valley. But the farm itself had come alive. Under a big sycamore the farmer was busy among his flock, and as I watched him, his wife came out to invite me in for a cup of tea.

'What is he doing?' I asked.

'Trimming the mud off their tails. They collect a powerful deal', she said.

She took me in the flag-stoned kitchen. Hams and sides of bacon hung from the rafters. She had just done her week's baking and the room smelt deliciously of new bread. Frances, her seventeen-year-old daughter, sat by the window while her mother talked about farming, the price of sheep, and other such matters. Frances had curly golden-brown hair, tied in a bunch at the back of her neck, a perfect complexion, and serious grey eyes under thickish black eyebrows. I wished some of our London girls, with their hard, thin, plucked ones could have seen her.

When the boys returned for the holidays I asked if they would like to come to the waterfall on the Lugg, and as they shared my passion for streams they needed no persuasion.

This time we took the train from Craven Arms to Llangunllo Station on a delightful little line, now closed I fear. A westward turn up a narrow lane brought us to a lonely farm set high on top of the hills. There seemed no one about except some hens who clucked at us from one of the ground-floor windows. Under a sycamore hung a long line of entirely *black* washing,—due, no doubt to a recent death in the family. It looked sombre and strange against the background of sunlit fields and misty blue hills.

After many a dip down and climb up we reached the waterfall. This was an immense success. The boys, very hot after their long hard walk, stripped off their clothes and placed themselves right under the fall. Their white bodies gleamed against the dark rocks. They laid trails of water-weed on their heads and these streamed down their shoulders in long green tresses, so that they looked like water-sprites. Unfortunately we stayed too long in this enchanting place and then dawdled to pick whinberries. The result—we reached the station just in time to see our train disappear into a tunnel in the hills. There was not another for two hours, so, after roaming for a while, we accepted an invitation from the station-master to sit in his tiny office. Now and then the telephone rang, and from our host's comments we learnt just where our train was at that particular moment.

'So she's just leaving Llandrindod is she?'

'She's got to Llanabister? So she'll be along presently, will she?'

The little train seemed in no hurry. She evidently enjoyed a leisurely journey through the hills and through another tunnel near Pennybout.

At last, very late, she came puffing along in the dark, and carried us back to Craven Arms.

Later, during another hot spell, because we had loved the Lugg near its source, we determined to see what its lower reaches could offer. So we stopped at Aymestrey, the next village to Wigmore, and, carrying bathing things, followed the river westwards through meadows where grew a host of autumn crocuses. A pool below a weir enticed everyone to plunge in as fast as they could tear off their clothes. Only Jill, not quite five, remained nervous. Running water still seemed more an enemy than a friend. She hovered near the bank, unable to trust herself to the inflated rubber ring that she wore round her waist. Suddenly there was a squeak of alarm and I saw her swept headlong down the current. Though swift, it was a very shallow current and I felt no great alarm, though I fancied she might herself be frightened. But I was wrong, the experience enraptured her. The squeak changed to gasps of delight, and she insisted on going down 'the rackets', as she called them, over and over again. The trick the river had played her turned her into a real Water Baby.

Afterwards, whenever I crossed the bridge at Aymestrey, I remembered that small white body being carried along the foaming water. Our bathe over, our tea on the banks over, all feeling cool and happy, we decided to go and look at the church. It is a rewarding church, and the boys were especially pleased by the ancient curved dark oak altar back, where Christ, uplifted in the centre, is attended by a cheerful-faced, very male sun on His right, and a serious woman-like moon, wearing a crescent-shaped hood, on His left. They also read out in loud chorus a long early 18th century epitaph to a local inhabitant, part of which told how, among many other qualities he was,

'Gentle to poore, respectful to the greate,
To kindred tender, and to equals sweete!'

My next visit to the Lugg and its neighbourhood was on a wild but beautiful April day, when Oliver and I motored westwards beside it, past Whitton, past the field where Owen Glendower won his victory and took the future Henry III prisoner, and on to where the river turns sharply northwards.

Here we left our car and followed a main tributary that has its source in a pool high in the hills. Black-headed gulls swirled and shrieked across it as we basked in the heather and watched the flashing of their wings reflected in the clear water.

On our way home, as we reached the lower end of the valley, the day changed and a huge cloud brooded over us, making the world dark and cold. So we were surprised to see a crowd of people gathered on the banks of the brook, at a place where it had evidently been widened for sheep-washing.

They were all very solemn and silent, and we were wondering why they were there when a deep voice boomed out—'I baptise you in the name of the Father, of the Son and of the Holy Ghost', and we caught a brief glimpse of water being poured from a pitcher over somebody's head. It was evident that we had walked straight into a Baptist ceremony.

We drew nearer and as we joined the crowd three people, standing waist-deep in the water, climbed up the bank—a girl and two young men, all wearing heavy black mackintoshes and gumboots. The girl shook the water, retriever-like, from her dark hair. Her eyes were shining and she looked amazingly gay and fresh, almost as though she had indeed been reborn. But the young men's faces remained solemn. Wisely, considering their wetness and the harshness of the wind, the three didn't wait for the rest of the service but hurried off for a feast at the little inn. The young men, infected by the girl's high spirits, joined in her talk and laughter. Was it the assurance of salvation that made them so cheerful now, or was it the anticipation of hot tea, dry clothes, and a bright fire?

But the crowd remained singing under the tossing trees. The men's deep voices followed us all the way down the lane.

It was not long after this that I heard more of these outdoor Baptisms from a patient of Tom's, a farmer's wife, whom I found busy rolling out 'pills for the gulls'—small pellets, rather like large orange pips, made from flour and pounded egg yolks. These, she said, accompanied by chopped goose-grass (or cleavers) are the best nourishment they can have. Young turkeys thrive on chopped nettles and dock leaves.

Then she talked of her old home in Wales, and showed me a photograph of a Baptist christening in a stream, which reminded me of the scene above Bleddfa.

'Does nobody ever catch cold?' I asked.

'Never', she said emphatically, 'It dunna matter how delicate they be. There was a poor cripple boy whose parents were scared to death about his Baptism, but he came out better than he went in. As to his body, I mean; his soul, too, you may be sure'.

Her son, who has acted in a play for me, came back just then from carting and shook hands without the customary hesitation in offering a dirty one. I'm sure he thought that it's the natural state of hands, as it surely often legitimately is.

The farm had a glorious view of Caradoc, the Stretton Hills, and Wenlock Edge, bluebell blue today, but firm and clear beyond the delicate green of budding trees and hedges. The geese formed a white wreath on the hillside.

128

The Teme rises in a narrow fold on the south of Kerry Hill, where it has a far livelier birth than our Brook in its peat bog. Streams scuttle down on either side to swell it rapidly. Alders, hazels, willow arch over it. To the north towers a high, richly wooded hill; to the south spread small lawn-like fields, grazed by innumerable sheep. Small farms begin to appear. A chain of villages with such pleasing names as Felindre, Beguildy, Llanvairwaterdine, Duthlas, Knucklas, are scattered along the banks, peaceful little places beside a peaceful river.

But, like all rivers that rise in these Border hills, the Teme can change its character with amazing speed. We heard of bridges swept away, and of one woman who looked through her cottage window to see both her cow and cow-house disappear down the river before her very eyes.

But for much of its length the Teme flows tranquilly along through the fields when no floods trouble it. Of course we knew it far less intimately than our own Brook. There was, however, one stretch which we dearly loved.

On an early Spring day Jill, a small friend, and myself were exploring a lane east of the junction with our Brook, when we noticed how sharply the land fell away to our right. We left the car and scrambled down to find ourselves in a deep gorge. On one side rose a high sandstone cliff, carved, grooved, bastioned, like the outer wall of some huge castle; on the other flowed a still fairly tranquil river. But suddenly it changed. The banks narrowed and steepened, and the river changed to a torrent, swollen, no doubt by recent heavy rains. Over great boulders and slabs of stone it plunged, leaving each with a fringe of white foam, and filling the air with its deep triumphant roar.

We moved now in a twilit world, breathing a delicious smell of good, damp earth, till we reached a weir, an old mill, and a house that was evidently lived in. Presently as the children climbed about the high wooded banks, a delighted cry rang out. Among the polypodies, the moss, the woodruff leaves, they had found a twig of Spanish chestnut glowing with scarlet elf-caps. For them it was a bit of pure magic. Our other happy discovery was an echo. We grew aware of it when we sheltered from a storm under a wide aqueduct, that carried an enormous volume of water from the Elan Valley to Birmingham. The children laughed because I had

129

slipped on a shiny stone and sat down hard. A peal of laughter sounded overhead. Entranced, they laughed again, and again, and always the echo seemed to triple their merriment so that the whole gorge rang with the sweet, clear notes.

'Roman Baths' was the next excitement offered by the Gorge. The boys found them on our map, and begged to go in search of them. As they scrambled high up the northern bank an excited shout reached me. Down they plunged through the undergrowth to lead me up to their discovery. Yes, there were the baths, buried among bushes; dank, dark, moss-grown. Stony steps led down to water in a stone basin. I felt strangely puzzled. I knew little about Roman Baths, but these, hidden in a sunless wood, struck me as distinctly odd. But, said the boys, if Mr. Bartholomew called them so, he must be right. When later I consulted a guide-book, my misgivings were justified. These baths had been built in the days when country gentlemen loved to embellish their estates with romantic ruins. To the same period no doubt belonged the Gothic castle that crowned the hill-top further down the Gorge.

My next visit was with Tom on a May evening, when trout rose freely, and his hands itched for a rod. A half-eaten salmon lying on a rock told of the existence of another kind of fish. Presently we met the man who lived in the little house beside the weir. Knotted about his throat was a red spotted handkerchief that matched the robin-red of his cheeks. I asked him about otters. His lad, he said, had seen one only yesterday slipping across the meadow as he drove his sheep to pasture. He himself had recently watched a pair racing after each other in broad daylight.

The light had grown dim by the time we entered the deepest part of the Gorge, and we picked our way carefully over slippery stones, stopping often to look down in hope of seeing an otter for ourselves, but in vain. It seemed that all the world except myself saw them.

Wild garlic flowers and clumps of primroses shone in the darkness, and their scent filled the air, along with that of herb robert and wet moss. Even if a bit of a fraud, the Castle looked truly imposing against the evening sky with mist wreaths curling round it.

When a year or so later I returned to the Gorge I stood watching a great spotted woodpecker give resounding taps on a tree, when the man who had talked about otters came by. He looked sad and different. There was no red handkerchief round his neck; no colour in his cheeks. Soon I understood why. His wife had died during the winter, and he and his son lived alone in the cottage by the weir.

''Tis nat'rul for the lad to be often out evenings', he said, 'so 'tis terrible lonesome now'.

I pictured him in the dark little house with the eternal sound of water in his ears and no woman to bustle round and cheer him with her talk.

When, over thirty years later, I returned eagerly to this much-loved place, the little house was in ruins, the weir collapsed, the Gorge sadly over-grown. No longer was it possible to stand under the aqueduct and listen to the echo of children's laughter.

Here I will add a foot-note about otters. After those years of frustration, we were living in a Dorset village where a narrow tunnel carried water from a brook at the bottom of our garden to what had once been a tanning mill. This tunnel passed right under our lawn. One day Oliver was mowing when suddenly he disappeared, machine and all, below the surface. One of the wooden sleepers that supported the turf had collapsed. After this a pool appeared right under my bedroom window. We decided to leave it for the present; a most fortunate decision, for soon afterwards I began to hear splashing sounds, far too loud for water-rats or small fish. Could they—oh, could they—be made by otters? The next night I fixed my bedside light, discreetly veiled, on the window-sill, and directly I heard the splashing again I crept from my bed and looked down into the pool. There was an otter, shining in the soft light, tossing an eel to her two cubs!

After that I watched otters several times, sometimes the mother and her young, sometimes a big dog otter. They seemed particularly to like thundery nights, frequent that summer. Eels came upstream more freely then. My long endeavours were rewarded. I could now watch the play from my private box. There was one gorgeous moonlit night when the otter and her cubs seemed made of liquid silver.

X

AWAY TO THE SOUTH

The wild hilly land south of Radnor Forest is always linked for me with a long, long drought, ten weeks of it, starting in March and going well on into May.

I first explored this piece of country on an April day when an east wind blew, the sun shone, and the earth was as dry as a bone. A steep path led me from the valley of the Summergill Brook to a high place where once a house stood. Bits of grey wall still thrust up through the undergrowth, and I traced the edges of the garden. A wealth of trees bounded it; sycamores in full blossom and musical with bees; a clump of fine Scotch pines, hawthorns, an apple-tree or two, all enjoying their freedom to spread as they pleased. Only a dejected box-bush looked as if it missed human society. As always when I light on a deserted homestead like this, I longed to find out who last lived there and why it had been allowed to fall into ruins. On account of the loneliness and remoteness, I supposed.

Below, the ground dropped steeply, and soon I found myself in a little cwm startlingly green and fresh after the parched hills. A tawny stream ran through the middle, and a row of bird-cherries dropped their white plumes over it. Newly-opened primroses covered the banks. As I paddled my hot feet and noted how full of birds and flowers it was, how cut off from the rest of the world, I felt, ridiculously, as if no one else had ever been there before. And then suddenly the harsh note of an axe shattered all this. A large hawthorn lurched forward and toppled slowly down the steep hillisde. A man holding an axe hastened its cumbersome roll with a shove, and another man with two horses and a chain waited for it at the foot of the hill. He bound the poor bush, covered with pearly buds that now would never open, and prepared to lug it away. Were *all* those thorns on the hillside to be cut down? I asked. Yes, all of them;

they were wanted for fencing. What did he call those flowering bushes beside the stream? 'Dog-trees', he said—because their berries were not edible, I supposed.

If, in this lower part of the cwm signs of drought were non-existent, it was a different story when I started to climb further into the hills. I followed the river-bed between banks that grew higher and rockier at every step, past little dried-up waterfalls where the stones were covered with dead grey moss. The body of a fox lay rigid at the water's edge, but he showed no signs of violence. Had he taken poisoned bait and struggled down for a drink I wondered?

The little cwm was now a deep ravine. The croak of ravens overhead led me up the course of a waterfall, and there on an ivy-covered crag above it I found a nest, but it was blocked by two large stones. Someone had been doing dirty work here. And it was such a beautiful place for a nest. After this the landscape changed again. The ravine grew shallower, the stream narrowed and filled up surprisingly. Cuckoos flew shouting from side to side. A snipe drummed, and a pair of sand-pipers tried to decoy me from their nest. They needn't have troubled; I never found it. For the first time since I met the wood-cutters, I saw another human being—a dark, rather ragged little girl paddling in the stream. I wanted to talk to her but she fled to join the two other children round the next bend. They also began to run as fast as their legs would carry them, stealing a backward look at me now and then till they were lost to sight.

When I got back to my car, well content with my day, a man with a lean, attractive face was hedging close by. Yes, the weather was grand for walking, but didn't my poor feet get tired on the hard, dry ground?

'Mine do', he said, 'I changes my boots as often as three times a day now'.

We parted with the hope that rain would fall soon, but the cool keen air and the rose-red sky gave no promise of it.

You must go to Ireland

My next visit to this country was with my friend the school mistress from Cascot. Still the same cold east wind blew, still never a drop of rain fell. We set off along the Builth road, and then turned off for Glascym by a lane that grew increasingly twisty and steep. Glascym is a tiny place deep among the hills. In the church porch hung large notice-boards affirming the rights of the parishioners of Glascym and adjoining parishes to enjoy forever the commons of Llanadegley, Rhos and other places 'for purposes of exercise and recreation'.

As we drank our tea beside a rough road high above the village, a farmer drove past in an ancient car and couldn't resist the chance for a chat. He walked to and fro in front of us with short quick steps and eloquent gestures. He reminded me of a squirrel with his bright beady eyes, the warm russet of his skin and his rapid, agile movements. His sudden bursts of fierceness, too, were those of a disgruntled squirrel. First there was this plaguey drought. That, following on foot-and-mouth disease, had halved the price of sheep from three pounds a year ago to thirty shillings. And as for wool, a friend had a lot stacked in a barn that wouldn't fetch a shilling a pound. And then here were all those restrictions to which farmers were subjected now-a-days. They were that irksome that he and his friends agreed they'd do better to just feed themselves and their families, and give up bothering about anyone else. And the taunts of folk from the towns! His eyes grew brighter and fiercer than ever.

'Seem to think that if we can live in such an out-of-the-way place as this, we must be a lot of boobies. God A'mighty, I'd like to see 'em tackle some of our jobs! And if we can't go to the pictures every week, we've minds of our own and a taste for music and such-like. There's my little boy, only four, took a prize at the Eisteddfod for saying his bit of poetry, and a man I know, who's worked all his life on a farm, has one of the best baritone voices in the country and came out first in the singing.

'I grant you some of us gets a bit narrow. There's my neighbour, the poor, little foolish fellow, come round and offer to fight me 'cos two of my sheep got into his blessed corn. Red-hot with it he was! For the Lord's sake, I said, don't let's fight about a thing like that, I sez. I'll pay you for the damage, I sez. Then he calmed down'.

He next turned the conversation to children being lugged away to school in the towns. I told him that we were discussing that now in our Women's Institutes. The mention of the W.I. roused the humorous side of him, as I find it almost invariably does with countrymen; a friendly humour, though.

' "Women in disputes", as we calls 'em,' he said. 'There was great bus-load of 'em went off last year to see the Bournville works or summat. And me and my pals says to each other, "If all the talk that goes on in that there bus today could be printed in a book 'twould be a mighty big one and no mistake".'

I smiled at the way he made fun of us women and our talking capacity, when here he stood, with words pouring from him, for over a quarter of an hour without stopping once. But we both enjoyed it. He was so alive, so proud of his own job in spite of present discontents. Before he went he asked what brought us to this part.

'We both like wild country', we said.

'Wild country! If that's what you want you'd best go to Ireland'.

'Ireland?' we echoed.

'I don't mean that old country you have in mind', he replied. 'Ireland's over there', and he pointed south; 'not many miles as the crow flies but a goodish way for us who haven't got wings'.

Then, to cut short further questioning he waved his hand, repeated mischievously, 'You go to Ireland!', hopped into his car and rattled away down the hill.

Ireland and Drought

For ten weeks the drought prevailed save for one small sprinkle of rain. The spring, that had seemed one of the most radiant I ever remembered, turned to desolation. All growth stopped. The half-starved sheep in the field beyond our orchard bleated piteously through the night. Young birds died in their nests for lack of food. A few miles away people queued for water in this land of rivers and springs, or plodded long distances to dwindling brooks. Flowers withered as soon as they had struggled up through the ground.

But suddenly we woke to a S.W. wind. Rain was surely on its way at last. Bright packed clouds rolled slowly above the hill. The sheep drifted down, the birds sang more loudly than for a long while. An overpowering wish to make the most of what might be our last fine day for a long while, and to find this mysterious place called Ireland, seized me.

I rang up my friend M. who responded to my appeal at once and caught the next bus. Except that it lay in this country south of Radnor Forest, I had only the vaguest idea of how to get to it. A lucky puncture brought more information. Two farmers who

gallantly changed our wheel gave us directions. These led us off the
Builth road along twisty stony lanes, thick with sheep and lambs
who had broken through their fences in a desperate search for food.
The lambs, to judge from their terror and surprise, might never
before have seen a car, and when we drew near a tiny school the
children, playing in the lane outside, bounded up the banks with the
same startled agility. We crossed a wide, shallow river, flowing at the
foot of a ridge of high hills, and drew up in the yard of a small
white farm. A young farmer, blue-eyed, swarthy, sturdy, left his
dusty harrowing and gave us willing permission to leave our car as
long as we liked.

'And while you're off on the hills maybe I'll have a run round in
her', he said.

However, it turned out that he'd never driven anything but his
pony-trap nine miles each week to Builth on market days.

Would rain come today? we asked. He glanced at the clouds,
still high above the hills.

'No, not today, but indeed tomorrow I think it will come'.

His voice was blithe at the prospect. When we looked back at
him from the steep hillside he was harrowing again, almost hidden
in a cloud of dust.

At about 1,200 feet we came upon the first of at least a dozen
ruined farmsteads, each built beside a spring, only all of them were
dry. The first house stood in a large mounded enclosure and was
ringed with sycamores, golden-green and humming with bees. A
brown owl fluttered on to a lower branch where he sat blinking at
us. As we stood staring back at him, I wished he could have told us
about the people who once lived up here. He looked so old and
wise, and those big yellow eyes must have seen so much. Close to
the heap of stones that had been the house was a great slab, large
as a tombstone, firmly rooted in the ground. Of the other ruined
houses seen as we climbed higher, some were as big as this one;
others, smaller, had obviously been very primitive dwellings, with
no enclosure, no big trees, only a few gnarled thorns. Could these
buildings set so high on the hills, so unfitted for winter, have once
been used only in summer time, we wondered?

At a point higher than the topmost ruin we at last found Ireland;
a keeper's cottage, surrounded by a small yard and a garden. Here
lived a really kind and friendly man, interested in other birds
beside his own game. He showed us where a ring-ouzel was nesting

in the heather, and a pet raven whom he'd rescued when it had fallen from its nest in a tree. Though not yet able to fly he lorded it over the domestic birds. A large cock strutted up to him as though to say 'I'll teach you your place, you young upstart!' but retreated hastily at the first movement of the big black bill; the turkeys, too, quailed before him. The keeper's wife clearly spoiled him disgracefully. She fed him from a spoon with mouthful after mouthful of biscuit meal, while the rest had what was left. Beyond the cottage a roadman was raking stones off a rough little road that led down into the next valley.

'Don't make it too good!' we begged him. 'Leave plenty of stones to discourage motorists'.

Perhaps it was unfair, that we, who didn't live here, should say that, but as a matter-of-fact the local inhabitants don't use cars. They walk, or ride, or drive. When we were 1,500 feet up we met a young man mounted on a fidgety pony who told us he was on his way to a new farm job. He carried a large suitcase balanced precariously across his knee.

There were few flowers in this high country. An unexpected one in the heather was a solitary wood anemone. Poor gallant little creature, how on earth had it got there? A seed carried on the wind, I suppose. The tormentil blossoms were even tinier than usual, and the wings of the yellow mountain pansy drooped wanly. Either the drought or the late frosts had brought disaster to a host of bumble bees; a rocky hilltop was strewn with their corpses for over a hundred yards. Only the birds seemed unaffected by the weather. Buzzards circled, ravens passed in unhurried fashion, curlews bubbled, grouse cackled.

As we dropped back to the farm by the river the promise of rain was darkening the nearer hills and bringing the further ones so close that all their little valleys and hollows showed up clearly. Our farmer was still at work, even dustier, but just as gay. He'd had a grand ride in our car, he said, and the drought was almost over.

We stayed the night at the Hundred House on the Builth road, and a cheerful stout little woman gave us a supper of bacon and eggs. When I went to bed the overcast sky darkened my little room prematurely and the wind kept pouncing in and flapping the curtains wildly. I jumped up to tie them back and saw the inn-keeper, only just visible in the twilight, digging desperately in his garden. Once or twice he glanced up at the sky, but still the clouds stayed sealed.

M. had to go home but I stayed on for another day among the hills. The wind had dropped; the world was grey and quiet as the sky slowly closed down on it. I drove along more small winding roads to Aberedw, which stands, just above the junction of the Edw with the Wye, among rocks and trees. We had often been near its source under Llanadegly Rocks when we tramped across the heather to Llanwehr Pool to watch black-headed gulls. At Aberedw I stopped to take a look at the little church and I blessed myself for doing so. You enter through a porch exquisitely carved with a pattern of clover leaves, and then find yourself facing an unforgettable chancel screen—so lightly built that it beautifully reveals what lies beyond, and from there, surprisingly, came the sound of a violin. A red-haired young man stood gravely playing St. Saens' 'Swan Song'. It was a nice quiet place to practise in, he said. His father was the vicar.

When he found I was going up into the hills, he told me to be sure to visit the Cave—the famous cave where Llewellyn hid himself during his last stand. But it was hard to find. He drew me a little map and gave me minute directions, which I promptly forgot, and also discovered I couldn't make head or tail of his map. However, for the present all I wanted was to roam in the wild rocky country above me. But before I left I found a delightful home-made epitaph in memory of an Aberedw builder. It ran:

> 'Now Cartwright with all his skill
> Can use no pencil, tool or quill
> As he on others oft did write
> Now others do on him indite
> But though he lies awhile in dust
> We have asu'rd hope and trust
> That man's great builder will him raise
> And build him up unto his praise
> Of his last resurrection
> In Christ, the living corner stone'

written, perhaps, by some simple predecessor of the young violinist's father.

As I climbed up, up, the rocky hillside, the wind began to growl in the crevasses. The clouds sank lower. Suddenly, after these ten dry weeks, my face was wet with small, soft rain. The sheep, scattered over the hillside, stood quite still, conscious that something supremely important was happening. The lambs, who could scarcely have had a chance to know what rain meant, continued nibbling the bushes. A little further on I reached a farm among the rocks. A woman drove some cows out of a barn, and then stood motionless and intent as the sheep, her face flung up to meet the rain. A flaxen-haired baby held on to her skirt. She told me she'd left kneading her bread because she remembered he'd never loosed the cows, and when she got outside she found the drought broken at last. For over a month they'd fetched every drop of water from the brook 500 feet below.

Was I looking for the Cave? She'd show it me with pleasure. I think she really welcomed an excuse for staying a little longer in the rain. So she put the baby to shelter in the barn and started off with me. When we looked back he was in the doorway stretching out his hands to catch the drops and laughing, his hair shining like a halo against the dark background. It was a good cave, dark and mysterious, well hidden among rocks and trees, but I was not tempted to enter and push my arm up a cleft in the roof like Francis Kilvert when he walked over from Clyro. Actual historical facts about Llewellyn's connection with the cave seem non-existent, but according to local tradition he came down from his castle among the rocky hills above Aberedw; fought the English in a skirmish; hid in the cave, and was killed in a haphazard way by a Knight as he knelt by a stream to drink. When his identity was discovered the English cut off his head and sent it for display in London. A sad tale of long ago, yet neither cave nor tale are what impressed themselves most clearly on my mind that day.

These were the little church above the river; the young man playing his fiddle; the gentle rain watering the hills after the long, long drought; the woman's wet, shining face and the baby's outstretched hands.

XI

SOME BIRDS OF THE BORDERLAND

If any real ornithologist happens to read this book he will know that I can lay no claim to that title myself.

But I love birds and watching birds, and in this chapter I try to tell of my contact with a few chosen ones in the Borderland.

Herons

Herons have always interested me from the day when, as a small child, I wandered alone across some water-meadows near my Wiltshire home and saw for the first time a strange, long-legged bird standing beside a little boggy pool. He looked so still, so intent, that I knew instinctively he must not be disturbed, so I crept away as quietly as I had come.

After life for some years in a waterless country, here were herons again on the banks of the Brook, and again I respected their stillness, their solitude. But meditative and philosophic though they might look, the sudden sharp turn of the head, the quick downward thrust of the neck, betrayed a single absorption.

Sometimes they hunted low over the fields for frogs. Our schoolmaster, fishing one day, found a hole in the bank full of frogs, reserved for future use, alive, but paralysed by a sharp nip on the back of their heads.

Whether through envy of their size, or because they fly so slowly, other birds seemed to hate herons, or, at all events, to delight in teasing them. Once I woke to hear a series of short, sharp barks, and looking from the window saw one flapping over the garden pursued by a trail of starlings. Another time, beside the Brook, a heron passed overhead pursued by half-a-dozen rooks cawing crossly.

At last a chance came to watch these birds more intimately.

On a cold, windless March day I left my car near a neighbouring village and wandered off across a piece of wide meadowland. Now and then a tiny snow-flake fluttered down on to the sparse brown grass, where no vestige of a flower, not even a daisy, was to be seen. The hedges were of uniform blackness. But the air quivered with curlews' voices, so that Spring hit the ear if not the eye. Suddenly I saw, at the foot of a steep hillside, a large pool, clear, silent, without a ripple to break the reflection of yellow rushes, purple trees, blue hill. Only when a coot swam across, leaving a double trail, was the surface disturbed for a moment.

But what really held me was a heron standing at the end of a narrow peninsula, and another flying from a wood of larch and fir at the foot of the hill. Through my binoculars appeared many long grey necks outlined against the dark trees; I counted no less than seventeen nests. As I hurried forward I don't know whose excitement was the greater, mine or the herons'. They left their nests and wheeled above me with sharp angry barks, squawks, and a noise sometimes like a faulty motor horn; sometimes a cross between a huge cock trying to crow and an owl to hoot. It was most peculiar. Or, with a wild flap of wings, one bird would chase another, whereupon the pursued would settle on a high branch and cluck furiously. Under the trees it looked as if a whole pot of white paint had been emptied. The ground itself was scratched and the moss uprooted in a search for grubs; here and there lay a delicate blue-grey feather. Seeing how unwelcome I was I had the good manners to take myself quickly away on that occasion. But of course I had to go back six weeks later, accompanied by Mrs. Mac, Tom and Oliver. Oliver, an excellent climber, swarmed up four trees. He found one empty nest, another with three eggs, and another with fledglings. He held out one for us to see and its gawky young head showed clearly above the rim of the huge nest. But Tom could not bear to look. He hated heights and was terrified that Oliver might slip, or that a rotten larch branch might snap.

Hung from a tree near the pool we found the limp corpses of a jay, a crow and a Little Owl. Mrs. Mac was deeply disturbed, and her mouth buttoned and unbuttoned itself in its own peculiar way. The rest of us were also grieved, but to a lesser degree. The jay is so handsome; the crow so clever; the Little Owl so beguiling. But all have villainous ways with small birds and their eggs.

A keeper whom we met soon afterwards justified the shooting of the crow—to us, if not to Mrs. Mac—when he told us that he had picked up twenty herons' eggs sucked by crows.

A year later, on an April day of peculiar radiance, Jill and I dropped from the great Iron-Age camp of Bury Ditches to the heronry. On the way down we stopped for a drink of water at a cottage beside a tiny stream, 'prill' as some of the older villagers would have called it. In the garden two fawn-coloured nanny-goats butted playfully at a black-and-white collie. The girl who answered our knock had extra long eye-lashes and a marvellous complexion. As she dipped up water from the stream one of the goats trotted up to be petted.

'We have all our milk from them', she said. Certainly it suited her.

A slight veil of mist had gathered over the heronry, but we counted twenty-eight nests. On the ground below lay scattered a great array of egg-shells. The young birds made themselves known by a sharp, metallic clucking, first from one nest, then another. Sometimes a mother gave an admonishing cry as though to order silence, an order which always seemed to be obeyed.

Once we looked up and saw through the network of branches the tall form of a mother surrounded by the heads of her children, all bobbing over the edge of the nest for a peep at us.

Not many of the parent birds left the wood on our arrival. Instead they poised themselves on the highest branches, or swung on some slender twig that looked incapable of bearing their weight— which is, however, very light for their size; only about three and a half pounds.

Since we were clearly doing no harm we sat down for a few minutes to eat an apple each. Overhead eight birds circled in the last rays of the setting sun. They looked immense and seemed made of pure gold. The beauty of the pattern of their wings against the sky was in describable.

And when we came out of the wood more beauty awaited us. Across a sky of palest green saffron clouds were floating, and this light was reflected not only in the pool, but in the brook that ran beside us. It looked such a gentle innocent little brook but in its waters two small children had been drowned, first one of only eighteen months and the following year another two years old. I heard the story from an old man in the village. His family had owned a small farm on the banks of the stream for over 100 years. A feckless step-sister and her children came to live there, with this tragic result. Only after the second death was a fence put up at the bottom of the garden.

The Heronry drew me at all seasons.

On a Summer afternoon several birds were fishing in the pool, while a number of coots seemed to be holding a regatta. With raucous cries and tremendous splashing they raced each other from end to end. Mallard and moorhens kept sedately aloof from all this wild behaviour. The herons flew away at my approach except one, who, with out-spread wings, watched me from the top of a tree.

In a cold spell in January a line of ducks came waddling over the frozen surface, trying to maintain their dignity but slipping about in comical fashion. A very white stoat chased a rabbit in the under-growth, but when he saw me he disappeared with a snake-like movement, and the rabbit skipped off in another direction. Up in the wood the herons' nests were full of snow. Seen from below, through a tracery of twigs, they resembled huge umbelliferous flowers.

During those dark days before the War I went to the pool for peace as well as for bird-watching. But there came a sad day when I realised I should never see my friends nesting there again.

In the strange winter that followed the start of World War number Two, all the trees stood ice-bound in a frozen fog. Dead wood pigeons sat glazed to the boughs. Every hip berry left on the bushes gleamed through a little glass coffin. The air was full of sharp reports that cut through the stillness like pistol shots as branches snapped and crashed to the ground.

With deep misgivings I set out for the Heronry. It was in ruins; the larches were skeletons; all the great nests lay scattered on the ground.

Ravens

Perhaps it would be wrong to say I felt affection for the Raven, but his glossy black body, his penetrating eye, the impression he gave of tremendous power, whether he was beating up into the sky, or watching one from a rock, all combined to fascinate me.

And he was linked with happy memories. The first is of a hot little walled-in garden at St. Malo, where two small girls watched entranced as a dear old bird shuffled about on the cobblestone in a peculiar dance all his own, while he whistled.

'Merrily danced the Quaker's wife,
Merrily danced the Quaker'.

His voice resembled that of an old toothless man singing through his nose.

The second memory belongs to a far later period, when on the cliffs of North Devon I first saw a raven somersaulting down the sky; a thrilling sight that took me entirely by surprise.

Years went by and still I had not set eyes on another. Then we came to our border country and Harry told me that ravens nested in Radnor Forest. See them and find a nest I must and would.

Once, on the Whimble, I heard a deep croak and saw a bird flying purposefully across the sky.

Once, on Llanedegly Rocks, the boys cried. 'A nest! A nest!' There, indeed, was a huge nest on the edge of the precipice, *but* it was full of wicked stones.

At last, one February day I set off for the Forest determined not to be beaten. A harsh wind blew; on the hills streaks of snow lay like scattered bones; the Whimble wore a white crown. But none of this weakened my resolution. I decided to seek news at a small inn, called Forest Inn, on the extreme southern edge. The landlord, a new-comer from the Rhayader district, could tell me nothing. But, he said, an old lady who had lived close by all her life, would surely help me.

He took me to her cottage, where she sat with a bible on her knee, a shawl round her shoulders, and a big quilted sun-bonnet to keep her head warm.

'Yes indeed, I know the Forest well. I've lived in it ninety year', she told us.

'Then mebbe you know where the ravens (ravvens he called them) build?' shouted the landlord—for she was very deaf.

'Ravvens?' she repeated blankly.

'Big black-birds', I yelled.

'Black-birds. Ah, there was a blackbird in the garden this morning', she said.

We gave it up. Outside the inn stood a little man in a long tight moss-green overcoat that had once been black, a battered bowler and an ash-stick in his hand. He looked shrewd and knowledgeable.

'Ravvens? Yes, you'll find 'em over at Llanevan. They've built there ever since I was a lad.'

I asked for directions. He pointed north across the hills with his stick. 'Yonder, in a great chasm. You must follow your nose'.

But the weather looked terribly stormy by this time. The wind had grown wilder and the sky and the hills as wild as the wind. It would be dark before I could get back. More snow might fall, I turned for home. The ravens must wait. But at least I now knew where to look for them.

Soon after that Winter made a ruthless return. A blizzard swept the countryside. Then one morning Spring burst on us, and I no sooner looked out of my window than the word 'Llanevan' leaped to mind.

The boys were home for the holidays. The time was ripe. Two hours later we were speeding to Forest Inn, where we left the car to start on a circuitous walk northwards over grassy uplands interspaced by bogs. Curlews called all round us, and a pair of buzzards soared overhead. After a few miles we came on the carcase of a dead sheep—victim no doubt of the blizzard. Now only bones and tattered fleece survived. Mightn't it indicate the presence of ravens? A few minutes later we saw ahead a deep dark gash in the hillside. Llanevan! And here indeed were the ravens. For scarcely had we reached the edge of the chasm than up started a pair, first one and then another. A quick search through binoculars revealed a nest on a rocky shelf under a thorn bush, full, so it seemed, of white foam.

The boys, in tremendous excitement, scrambled up the crevasse and announced young birds. I followed along the top and looked down at three very pink, newly-hatched babies and a broken blue egg-shell, all lying in a bed of sheeps' wool. One good look and we conscientiously hurried away, but it was some time before the parents ceased to watch us—first both of them, then only one, presumably the father, who kept sweeping overhead in wide circles till finally he dropped on top of the cliff opposite the nest and kept his eye on us till we were safely away.

Llanevan Gorge was a thrilling place, wild and craggy, with a torrent at the bottom and lots of small waterfalls. The boys, blissfully happy, made dams. I knew we should often return there.

Next year, in April, I went alone. Though a cutting wind blew, the sun burst out at intervals and great bird-like clouds flew across the sky. Again I was thrilled to see the two ravens shoot up from the ravine at my approach. The nest was deeper now and more cup-shaped. Two eggs lay in their bed of sheeps' wool. All round on the cliff top the dark crow-berry bushes were lit up by little coral pink flowers.

The following March, after three weeks of wild north winds and snowstorms, Thomas and I drove to the Forest between drifts that were often two or three feet deep. The Whimble was white, ghostly, strangely remote. Snowflakes fluttered round us as we set off across the hills. When they ceased for a moment a burst of yellow light revealed a buzzard hovering moth-like above the grass. Though the snow was now over our gumboots we wouldn't give in till we had peered into the chasm. Alas, the nest was full of snow, and no ravens appeared. The ravine seemed a gaping black mouth, and the tinkle of the stream the only sound.

But in May there were three fully feathered young birds, who seemed to fill the whole nest. Two faced in one direction and the third the opposite way, so that they fitted in neatly.

Next Spring we again found the nest occupied.

In the fourth year we approached Llanevan, on a fine but blustery day, by a path just opposite Llandegely Rocks. At the bottom of the gorge a farmer was tossing hay to his cattle at a small farm beside the stream. We would like to have talked to him but felt he might not welcome an interruption.

Soon two ravens appeared on our right, just where a small steep chasm cut out of the main gorge. Could this mean they had changed their nesting site?

At all events we were half-prepared for the deserted nest full of last year's wool, grey and dirty now, that we found at the old site. Back we headed for the top of the smaller chasm through a thick growth of crowberry and whinberry. Directly we approached, the ravens shot up and sailed high overhead, and the male did two splendid somersaults down the sky. No sign of a nest appeared at first, but as we moved lower I noticed white droppings on nearby rocks. A shout from Oliver proclaimed one on a ledge under a rowan. Two young half-fledged birds made a splash of vivid colour, their rosy flesh half covered with blue down, their wide-open mouths a burning carmine. But a newly-dead lamb lying in the chasm just below them with blood still oozing from its mouth troubled me. The farmer we had seen might well feel the ravens his enemies if he found the lamb. Yet it seemed more probable that it had slipped over the precipitous edge, and, battered by its fall, presented an easy prey, than that it had been carried there. I earnestly hoped the farmer was too busy ever to walk this way. It was a beautiful nest set among a wealth of small flowers.

We hovered about for a short while, wishing we had something to drop into those gaping red mouths, while the parents swore at us from above. Once we hid ourselves and hoped to surprise them actually feeding their babies, but they were too sharp for us.

The farmer was standing at his gate as we passed on our homeward journey, so I raised the subject of the ravens. 'Did outsiders persecute them at all?' I asked tactfully.

'Yes', he told us. 'Young chaps on motor bikes from the town come along and take the fledglings because they learn to talk so clever'.

That was a danger I hadn't reckoned with. 'Couldn't they be prosecuted?'

'Mebbe, but I canna be bothered'.

'You're not afraid for your lambs?'

'No. Mebbe the ravens 'ull take a sickly one now and again—one that 'ud a died anyways'.

I felt relieved. They were safe from him at all events. But the thought of those predatory young males on motor bikes was disturbing. . . . Of course there was that old raven who had sung and danced in the garden at St. Malo, but that was so long ago, and not many captives could be as happy as he.

Ravens at Pistyll Rhaiadr

'You should to to Pistyll Rhaiadr', said an old naturalist. 'Ravens used to build there years ago and very likely still do'.

It was a long but worth-while journey into Montgomeryshire. A magnificent waterfall pours in two stages over a perpendicular cliff into a wide stone basin, arched over by a rock. Years later I was enthralled by a Samuel Palmer picture of it. Beside it our beloved Water-Break-Its-Neck would look almost insignificant.

At first we were so fascinated by the rush of water, the clouds of spray, the foaming pool, that we forgot the ravens. When they came to mind we searched the near-by cliffs in vain for the sign of a nest.

Down in the valley two haymakers told us, however, that ravens still built there, but it was a tricky place to find. Up till a few years ago, said they, a London gentleman came every year and gave a handsome sum to be lowered by rope to the nest, from which he would take the whole clutch of eggs. Thank heaven, the wretch —my epithet, not theirs—no longer paid his hateful visit.

We spoke of the waterfall.

'Ah', said one, 'you did ought to see it when there've been a frost and an east wind. 'Tis a grand sight then—all frozen and twisted into such shapes as you'd never believe'.

Soon after this an old-parson stopped to talk to us.

'Oh yes', he said. 'Not ravens only but peregrines too, only I fear they've left us. Many's the time', he continued, 'have I helped to lower a man down the cliff, but not to take eggs. No indeed. But to rescue a sheep or lamb'. He came from the neighbouring town of Llanrhayader where, he was proud to tell us, the Bible had first been translated into Welsh in the reign of Queen Elizabeth.

We never found the ravens' nest, but we had seen the waterfall and met this true country parson.

Kites

For years I had longed to see a kite, but since it was now so rare a bird, I felt little hope. A middle-aged village man remembered one above the Rock of Woolbury when he was a lad. And a bird-lecturer talked of their fastness in the Welsh hills, but rightly gave no detail. (Later, however, I found he was on the ornithological Black List as one who every year actually robbed a kite's nest of all its eggs.)

Then one October day arrived an exciting visitor—no less than the official kite-watcher for their last stronghold in Britain; Breconshire. She had heard how I loved birds and rambling on the hills. It seemed that young kites sometimes stray far from their birthplace, and she wanted a number of people to keep a watch along the Shropshire borders, and to send word of any that were seen. Would I find volunteers living in likely spots who would report to me? Of course I consented with alacrity, and she suggested I should take her westwards for a tour of inspection across Clun Forest and on into a tangle of hills on the other side of the Teme, which might be rewarding country.

The drive was one I shall never forget, partly because of my visitor's marvellous sight (she spotted a flock of golden plover quite a quarter of a mile away); partly for all she told me of kites and their habits; partly because of the kind of country we passed through along little roads where sometimes we opened as many as ten gates, up and down the hills, under tawny oak woods, on that perfect autumn day. My companion would point her finger at some north-facing wood and say, 'That is the kind of place they love'. I felt convinced I should soon either see a kite myself or receive a report of one. Mentally I affixed the letters K.W.S.B. to my name—Kite Watcher for the Shropshire Borders. We wound past lonely farms, where some of the people looked a little gloomy or sad. But a dark, gay-looking girl in a scarlet overall, who was feeding a flock of gobbling white ducks, flashed a smile at us.

When we had turned left for Knucklas along a forsaken little road and climbed to 1,200 feet and looked back at Radnor Forest, deep violet against a rose-red sky, my Kite Lady pointed at it and said, 'That's a place to watch, remember'.

We dropped through a succession of woods that grew ever more shadowy, and before we reached Knucklas darkness enveloped us.

Torrential rain stopped me from setting out immediately to establish Kite watchers, but one bright day about two weeks later, I took Mrs. Mac and a bunch of stamped post-cards bearing my name and address to that promising country west of the Teme. At a farm a mile or so from Felindre we asked the farmer, just off on his pony, if we might leave our car.

'Oh yes', he said, 'you can put it in the fold'. His jolly fat wife joined us and talked hard while we unpacked ourselves. She laughed so heartily at everything we said that we felt remarkably witty. She told us to follow 'the wrack' (a rough road) beside a brook into the hills, or, so swelled it was with all the rain, it might prevent our going 'where we'd a mind to'. So we followed this rollicking brook; skirted an oak wood, and tramped uphill till the wrack died on us, crossed a turnip-field and a bit of heath-land, and reached a high lonely farm. The owner was hiding behind the door of a shed, but when he had decided we looked not too alarming, out he came. His farm was called Llannerch, he said, and his name was Jones.

He was a youngish sad-faced man.

'Oh yes, 'twas beautiful country in summer no doubt, but in winter terrible lonesome and often cut off by snow'.

He'd been in the army once, and in Glasgow for six months, and 'my word that was a different place to this!'

He wished he was back in the army now—'you did see a bit of life anyways'. I told him how I was seeking news of kites. He saw lots of buzzards, but couldn't say he'd ever seen one with a forked tail. But only a day or two ago there'd been a huge great bird,

149

something like a buzzard only much bigger—'big as a turkey almost'. He'd never seen such a great bird before. It had perched on a tree only a few yards away and he saw a lot of white on its under-parts and on its head. Naturally this filled me with excitement. It was not an owl, but fluffier than a hawk. What *could* it have been?

His face brightened as he talked about the bird, but soon the gloom returned. House and farmyard alike looked desolate and tumble-down. It belonged, he said, to Lord Dunsany (Dunseeny he pronounced it). Yes, he might well be one who wrote books. Certainly he was Irish. He never troubled to visit his farm. Mr. Jones' voice grew bitter now.

I told him I should return before long with my bird-book to see if he could identify that strange bird. We left him and went round to the front to ask his wife for a drink of water, but nobody answered our knock. I think she was hiding. The window was blocked with rubbish, but under it, to redeem the squalor, grew a mass of cream chrysanthemums.

The real glory of the place was on the other side, whence you looked over miles of hill country and of glowing woodland.

It grieved us to think that our poor farmer was probably too oppressed by his poverty and the condition of his farm ever to look beyond it.

Now as we went S.E. over the heath, we saw another farm, in a little hollow, with the Beacon bold and dark behind it.

We ate our lunch under a hedge and watched a tall old man come out of the house and wander up the field. Soon he was joined by a young one carrying stakes. Another youth led out two horses, one with a piebald saddle round his middle, loosed them and joined the fencing party. Two hungry, timid dogs watched us from a little distance, till one summoned enough courage to creep up and accept a few bits of bread; the other was too scared.

When all the food was gone we approached the fencers almost as timidly as the dogs had approached us. The youths looked up, then glumly resumed work. The old man took not the slightest notice, till our hesitating 'Good day' forced him to raise his eyes; his expression was definitely hostile. We asked the name of his farm. 'The Bwlch', he said and continued to drive a stake into the ground. But I was not to be defeated. Was he interested in birds? He looked at me with growing suspicion. No. There were no birds here at all. (A lark was singing not far away.) No, he'd never even seen a buzzard and indeed, his bleary, red-rimmed eyes looked as if they never lifted themselves to the sky.

'The only thing we see is rabbits', he grumbled, 'and they do a mort of mischief, blast 'em!'

He admitted they were fetching one-and-fivepence a pair, or even sometimes one and tenpence. This was because they were used in making gas-masks. *How*, we didn't quite understand. We wished the old boy would have allowed us a word with his sons, but they worked on, withdrawn and silent. I think they stood in awe of their father, as well they might.

Our course now took us westwards along the hillside, through the woods down to a stream and up to a pleasant farm topping the next hill.

All seemed deserted when we tried for the customary glass of water. Evidently, from the pails of distemper standing by the door, the house was being done up. Then a painter came out.

'I'll reach you a drink', he said and dipped a glass into a bucket. As we drank we asked about six holes, each some eighteen inches square, in the yard wall. 'Goose-cubs', he told us, 'for geese to nest in. Many old farms hereabouts have them.'

On our way down we met a handsome, bright-faced boy coming up the hill and I sounded him on birds. Yes, he often saw buzzards and promised to watch out for any with forked tails. His name, which I scratched with a hairpin on a visiting card, was Helvet Bevan of Llanrhys. He in his turn accepted a kite card.

As we returned on the west side of the valley, the woods opposite looked enchanting in the low light. Many trees were now bare, but larches and oaks still flamed. A buzzard hovered over the highest hill in a tawny sky.

That farmer at Llannerch and his strange bird often came back to my mind during the next two weeks, and on a cold day in early December I set out with a friend to talk to him again. We climbed through woods deep in shadow to bright sunlight and sparkling snow. Clouds like enormous bubbles rested on the Beacon. Mrs. Jones again refused to answer our knock but Mr. Jones appeared and welcomed us almost warmly. He couldn't ask us in, he said, because the bad weather had put the house all in a muddle. So we leaned against a henhouse for a chat, surrounded by gobbling turkeys, which, said he, a dealer from Knighton had already bought at one and tenpence a pound. I'd come armed with my bird-book and tried to get him to identify his bird. He repeated that it was as big as one of his turkeys and had a lot of white about it. He shook his head at all my illustrations. He had seen it sitting on a tree some fifty yards away. His face lit up as he talked about the bird, which had evidently been quite an event in his monotonous life, but after-wards looked more dejected than ever.

'Not much of a life up here. You're welcome to the view'. He'd been ill with asthma since we saw him, and his little boy had had his adenoids out in Shrewsbury Infirmary, but was now home.

'We don't loose him out much'.

Poor child, we thought, looking at the cramped little house and the tightly closed windows. From one a small white face peeped at us. The whole aspect of man and farm alike struck me afresh as wretchedly poverty-stricken. We felt deeply sorry for him and wished there was something we could do. We even thought of writing to Lord Dunsany. I had recently seen his play 'If'. 'If only he could see this place', I thought.

In contrast to the drab, untidy farm the landscape looked startlingly beautiful. As we walked back down the valley the lower larch-woods were in shadow but the higher trees caught by the setting sun burned like torches.

At home I hunted diligently in another book and almost convinced myself that the bird at Llannerch must have been an Osprey. After all, the farm was less than 40 miles from the sea in a bird-line.

To the real Kite country

In mid-February my Kite friend decided that I must see a kite for myself and invited me to her home on Lake Llangorse—a converted school built in Gothic style. I had driven there in wind, rain and sleet, and it was heaven to sit down to tea beside a blazing log fire.

Next day, in bitter wind but no rain, we motored to Llandovery, and then on beside the Towy to a farm where kites had lately roosted. The farmer, red-cheeked, shrewd, genial, told us that the evening before he had seen eight birds sailing in. But today, because of the driving east wind, it might not be so good. We sat ourselves down on the hillside. Suddenly my companion cried, 'Look! Over there!' and I saw my first kite fly low along the hillside. We watched him through our binoculars for some minutes, rising, falling, gliding above the bracken. The moment I'd long waited for had come. I was so enchanted that I felt warm right through, though a minute before

I'd been shivering. I saw the Y-marking on his back clearly, and his forked tail. When we wandered up the side of the wood he appeared silently just above us, hovered over the trees for a moment, then swooped down among them. This he repeated many times. He must have been after the little birds who had gone early to bed.

It was now 5 p.m.—roosting time—so we joined our farmer. The relentless wind set us both shivering again even when wrapped in rugs, but he, in a thin old coat, seemed oblivious of the cold. Suddenly he pointed out another kite flying slowly not far away, and I had a grand view of it against the hillside. The bracken, seen through the evening mist, was the colour of a dog rose. A third bird appeared momentarily, but our farmer thought they would choose a more sheltered wood that night.

When too dark to see, he took us in to the kitchen fire, for tea, Welsh-cakes, and black-currant jam.

The next day we sought news of kites in still remoter spots. And at each farmhouse where my friend's allies lived we went in for a chat. One farmer, on whose land a kite nested each year, told of the frightful cunning shown by egg-collectors. One day, in the middle of the last nesting season, he and his shepherd noticed a man slinking up the valley towards a nest. When they shouted at him he turned back, but they kept their eyes on him until he was out of sight. An hour or two later the shepherd observed him creeping back under cover of a hedge. He and the farmer closed in on him. He knew for certain that this stranger was a certain unscrupulous collector who had been seen in the village recently.

'Sorry sir, but this is private land and you can't go that way', said our farmer. The man simulated rage and indignation. 'What's the country coming to if a man can't take a quiet walk without being set on? Never heard of such a thing. It's damnable. I shall go on. I'm doing no harm'.

'We know the likes of you only too well', said the farmer. Then he and his shepherd stepped straight in front of him.

'You try to go one step further and my shepherd will use his stick on you, and that's the truth'.

Swearing and muttering, the intruder retreated down the valley, followed at a discreet distance by the other two, till they had seen him well away.

These egg-collectors were often the most desperate and relentless people. Two young men who were guarding a nest had their hut burned to the ground in revenge. Such high prices were offered for the eggs of the kite that a bonus of £25 had to be paid from the Kite Preservation Fund for every nest where young were safely reared.

My first kite news came in January of the following year from Cwm Gurwen near Bleddfa. Contact with the eye-witness, a Forestry man, proved impossible, but Oliver and I went up into the Cwm to look for ourselves; through a firwood, through a larch plantation, along the foot of some funny deeply grooved little hills called the Riggles, and on to the top of Llethr Dhu, 2,000 feet up. Though we had seen no sign of frost below, here, under a nipping wind, the palings were fringed with frozen drops, and the long pale grass was ice-tipped. The kok-kokking of grouse broke across the heather and a buzzard circled up the sky.

A lively young ram ran at me on our way down, but Oliver warded him off with a stick. We saw no kite, but found an admirable place for future duck-races in an exciting little ravine called Rocky Dingle.

A little later came a report of a kite near New Radnor, and this time I actually saw him for myself, beating his way slowly along a slope on the southern outskirts of the Forest. He looked magnificent in the sunlight against the dead bracken and the dark trees.

Though less often than I could have wished, news of kites continued to filter through to me at times. The friendly keeper at Ireland sent word that he often had three flying round his house; one, a young one, of extra large size. This was in June. Early next Spring news came of kites seen at a keeper's cottage called Black Yatt, above the western end of Cwm-y-bont. Off I set with a friend to Cwm-y-bont, where the stream was in full spate. We picked our way with difficulty along the slippery stones, and climbed to a little coal-black house (tarred against the weather) high above the ravine. The keeper's wife and daughter had just returned from wooding, and asked us in. Her husband would be back soon, she said. She had an enormous goitre on her neck and she said she often got terribly depressed. As we looked out through the small window at the wild landscape and heard the wind growling round the house we understood that life up here might be difficult for such a one as she. But she talked cheerfully, and seemed pleased to see us. The little room darkened as we talked and the hills too, but still there was no sign of the keeper. I went outside with my binoculars half hoping that a kite might fly by.

When I went back to the kitchen the wife looked out and cried 'There he is!'

I looked where she pointed into the twilight but saw only what seemed a big thorn bush. Oddly it drew nearer, and finally turned into a man bowed under a load of brushwood. I joined him as he unloaded himself. He was an East Anglian and a bit on his guard against me for a moment, but soon relaxed. Yes, he saw the kites constantly, three of them always close together, and one a great big bird. This tallied with what the keeper at Ireland had told me, but that was nine months ago, and it was hard to think it was the same trio. They often hunted, he said, over Llanwenny woods, off the Builth road.

We looked for them the next morning in vain, but at least I had more news to send to Breconshire. That was the last time. The coming of War ended the kite recording that had taken me into such wild, remote places.

Black-Headed Gulls

Away to the south of Llandegley Rocks, in the middle of a wide stretch of heath, and close to the source of the Edw, lies a lonely pool, where, people told us, the black-headed gull breeds freely. On a day late in April Tom and I went to it. When we were still quite a hundred yards away enormous excitement broke out. Hundreds of white wings flashed and shrill cries tore the air. More gulls flew in from various rocky outposts to join the medley. Sometimes the flock dropped suddenly to the water, and then it seemed as if we were walking straight into a snowstorm—a snowstorm made up of huge whirling flakes. When we reached the edge of the pool a cloud of birds flew off to keep watch from chosen vantage points.

In the marshy land round the pool, and among the rushes in the water, we counted 145 nests, and I'm sure there were others undetected. All contained eggs; no babies visible. Great restlessness prevailed all the time. Some gulls would sit for a minute and then rise again, and in would fly the watching birds with renewed clamour.

We had been told that a wholesale robbery of the nests by boys from Llandegly takes place each season, and that omelettes and scrambled eggs are eaten in every cottage.

In our ignorance we exclaimed, 'How wicked!'

But when an ornithologist had explained what a horrid toll of other birds' eggs, and of baby birds, the black-headed gull takes, we felt more doubtful.

Yet all the same when we met two boys leading a donkey carrying a pair of large pannier baskets, and found that they would be filled with eggs we could not help feeling sad.

As we looked back at wild flashings of wings and heard the lamentable cries we wished we could have saved their nests. But the boys had the law on their side.

XII

THE COMING OF WAR

When the summer of 1938 was drawing to a close and the shadow of war loomed dark, the homeward journey after a long drive through Radnor Forest, through Builth, through the kite country round Llandovery, to fetch Jill from a little seaside place called Ty-Gwyn, brought back memories of a period preceding another war.

Poised high on the cliff top I saw the same little white church near which I and a friend had slept in sleeping-sacks in the Summer of 1914. Only then, young, and not deeply concerned with foreign affairs, neither of us were conscious of the disaster that threatened. We had started off gaily from Gwbert-on-sea on a hot summer day, had lugged those damnably heavy sleeping-sacks (of thick canvas lined with sheeps' wool, which, without R. L. Stevenson's donkey to carry them, we soon discarded); had laid them on the cliff top not far from that little white church and gone to a farm to ask for milk. The farmer's wife said before we left, 'Will you please listen to my little girl say the Lord's Prayer in English? 'Tis grand how she does it'.

Then a mite in a white flannel night-gown knelt down and murmured a string of words that might have been the Lord's Prayer, or equally a nursery rhyme, or anything else as far as we were concerned.

We took our milk, and spent a blissful night just above the sea. Away at Sarajevo an Arch-Duke was murdered that night.

Twenty-four years later, while we made this other Welsh journey under a second shadow of which we were all desperately conscious, we stopped for a supper of eggs and bacon at a little place called Beulah, between Llanwystyd Wells and Builth. While we waited for it, we wandered out and watched the dim figures of haymakers, both men and women, moving about in the twilight, raking up the last bits of hay, loading the last cocks on to a cart. Whether it was that evocative name Beulah, or some line from his poems, or the pale

157

bending figures, I don't know, but the scene took on a strangely Blakeian quality, and brought a moment's special kind of comfort. The crisis passed, but left me stunned and anguished as though struck by a sharp blow on the head. Czechoslovakia had been abandoned.

Then, just about a year later, this blacker cloud piled up. Hitler's evil presence was never far away no matter where we went. Again, in the midst of the creeping horror, a haymaking scene seemed endowed with added beauty and significance. Jill and I had gone in the evening to the Weir Pool in Holly-Field Cow-Pasture, and there again in the dusk we watched the haymakers gathering up the last of the hay, saw our Hill darken, heard the white owl who nested in a hollow willow-tree let out his long strange cry.

A little while before this there was another pleasant happening in the midst of the gloom. In the village street I met a funny, unusual turn-out. This consisted of an ancient little hooded cart drawn by a piebald pony. In the driver's seat sat a dark, huddled man and a lively-looking woman. Perched at the back was a monkey in a scarlet coat, grimacing at me. On the hood of the van was chalked in big letters, 'Come and see Pamponi's Mammoth Show Tomorrow', What a happy touch was that word 'Mammoth'!

Well, I thought, this promises to be fun. And so it turned out when we went to the Village Hall next evening. The man, an Italian with a wooden leg, and his wife, gave spirited dialogues, recitations, and duets. The monkey played various tricks and finally—and this fairly brought the house down—rode on the pony's back up and down the hall, sometimes grasping its mane, sometimes facing the tail, and rolling his little yellow eyes mischievously at us as we clapped and roared with laughter.

'Just you wait till I play a few tricks on you!' he seemed to be saying. 'I'll give you something to laugh at!' His chance came next day. The Pamponis had obtained permission to camp in a neighbouring orchard, and several people visited them next morning bringing small country offerings.

I was pottering in the garden when I heard shrill screams. I ran to the orchard in time to see a stout little woman being chased by the piebald pony. She had just taken refuge behind an apple-tree when the monkey, hidden among the branches, proceeded to drop apples on her. Before I could come to her rescue Mrs. Pamponi hurried out, drove the pony off and caught the monkey.

They were full of apologies, particularly as their visitor had brought a gift of butter and eggs, some of which I'm afraid were broken. She was panting and very pink, but soon recovered over a cup of tea. Unfortunately this interesting couple left before I had the talk that I'd hoped for. When I hurried round later they had already gone. So now I shall never know any more about them. But they brought a flash of gaiety in the darkness such as I'll never forget.

As Billeting Officer I now was kept busy finding homes for the coming flood of evacuees. Most people seemed willing, but incredulous that war would really come. When I had done all I could, I decided to carry out a long-cherished plan before it was too late; to camp for a night with Jill in Clun Forest.

In the late afternoon of a gorgeous day we set off in the car with tent, sleeping-sack, and food, and chose the top of the hill above Sarn, where Oliver used to perform his capers.

Heather was in full bloom, whinberry-pickers busy. After tea Jill collected sticks and dug a trench for a fire in a safe spot. I sat on the edge of the steep escarpment and tried to paint some airy clouds—very indifferently but with supreme contentment. The browsing sheep, the slow-drifting clouds, the whinberry-pickers passing home down the slope with laden baskets, a young moon hanging over the heather, Jill absorbed in her job and murmuring at intervals 'I'm so happy!' (and she is not usually given to expressing her emotions)—all this for a little while drove Hitler away.

It grew cold as darkness fell and I actually was glad to sleep in the tent—I who have always scorned one and preferred the open ground. But through the wide opening I could see the misty twilit hills. We fell asleep murmuring how nice it was, and how we'd get up at sunrise and roam about before breakfast.

But instead we woke to find ourselves, the hills, everything, wrapped in cold fog. The light when it came was a dead light. Nothing moved. No curlews called.

'Soon it will lift', we kept saying, but it never did—at least not till nearly two in the afternoon.

All our happiness on the previous evening was damped down by this gross impenetrable gloom. When we decided that home would be the better place the car herself was so cold and depressed that she refused to start. We tried to boil a kettle of water to encourage her, but the sticks were too damp. At last a kind boy walking with his dogs came to our rescue, dried the plugs, blew up the fire, produced hot water for the radiator and got us going. But it was a sad anti-climax, and as we drove home I had a feeling that the evening before had been the happiest we shall know for a long time; that the cold fog was typical of what lay ahead.

Five days later war was declared. Thomas, a Territorial, had already been called up. Oliver must follow before long. Our happy, carefree rambles over the hills, up the river valleys, were over. But the Hill and the Brook and our country friends remained.